She Read to Us
in the Late Afternoons

Also by Kathleen Hill

Still Waters in Niger
Who Occupies This House

She Read to Us
in the Late Afternoons

❧

A Life in Novels

Kathleen Hill

Kathleen Hill (signature)

DELPHINIUM BOOKS

First Edition

Jacket and interior design by Greg Mortimer

Library of Congress Cataloguing-in-Publication Data is available on request.
ISBN 978-1-88-328572-2
17 18 19 20 21 RRD 10 9 8 7 6 5 4 3 2 1

Lucy Gayheart was published as "The Anointed" in *Doubletake* (1999),
© 1999 by Kathleen Hill

An earlier version of the chapters entitled *Things Fall Apart* and *Portrait of a
Lady* was published as "Portrait" in the Ploughshares Solo Series (2014),
© 2014 by Kathleen Hill

An earlier version of the chapters entitled *Madame Bovary* and
Diary of a Country Priest was published as "Avesnes: Reading in Place" in
Michigan Quarterly Review (1998) 37, 1, © 1998 by Kathleen Hill

An earlier version of the chapter entitled *À La Recherche du Temps Perdu* was
published as "Reading with Diana" in *The Yale Review* (1998) 72, 2,
© 1998 by Kathleen Hill

Letter from Diana Trilling: Copyright © 1975 by Diana Trilling, used by
permission of The Wylie Agency LLC.

Travel by your reading all the way to paradise and sigh over what was lost.

— Peter of Celle, *On Affliction and Reading*

For Clifford

Contents

"The Angle of a Landscape"

— Emily Dickinson

And the child standing on her head in the grass in front of the house, looking at it upside down? Who sees that the two tall brick chimneys are the legs of the house, holding it up against the sky? That the chimney pots are its two round feet? She had always thought that the windows sticking out from the slates of the roof looked like eyebrows, peaked in the middle. Now she understands that instead they point to the underside of the house, that place between the legs.

This is the same child who, when she grows tired of fussing around in the grass this September afternoon, squashing the red yew berries and pulling the yellow stickiness between her fingers, goes to sit on the front steps, the one at the top with the black iron numbers nailed to its broad base: 122. It is here, sitting in the warm sunlight, that she picks up the reader she'd left there when she got home from school, the one she'd asked the teacher to give her from the cupboard in her first-grade classroom. Thinking of nothing in particular, the book open on her lap, she sees all at once how it is that the words taken one at a time give you a single thing to think about—a girl, a boat, the sea—but that taken together, in clumps, they tell a story. The same story the pictures tell: a girl named Alice is walking one day beside the blue sea.

Looking up from her book the child sees how everything in the afternoon around her is holding still—the boy slouched on his bike, arms hanging loose at his sides, the black cat crouching low on the wall across the street, even the fly on the page, rubbing its hind legs together. They must be inside a story, too, but she doesn't know what it is.

Lucy Gayheart

———

*My harp is tuned to mourning. And my flute
to the voice of those who weep.*
—Job 30:31

I

In Miss Hughes's seventh-grade music class, we were expected to sit without moving finger or foot while she played for us what she called "the music of the anointed." At a moment known only to herself, Miss Hughes opened the album of records ready at her elbow and, tipping her head from side to side, cautiously turned the leaves as if they had been the pages of a precious book. When she had found the 78 she was looking for, she drew it from its jacket and placed it on the spinning turntable. But before lowering the needle she took a moment to see that we were sitting as she had instructed: backs straight, feet on the floor, hands resting on our darkly initialed wooden desktops.

While the record was playing, Miss Hughes's face fell into a mask, her mouth drooping at the corners. A small woman in high heels, she stood at attention, hands clasped at her waist, shiny red nails bright against her knuckles. She wasn't young, but we couldn't see that she was in any way old. The dress she wore was close-fitting. Often it was adorned by a scarf, but not the haphazard affair some of our teachers attempted. Miss Hughes's scarf was chosen with care, a splash of blue or vermilion to enliven a somber day, and was generous enough to allow for a large, elegant loop tied between her breasts.

Most of us had turned twelve that year and were newly assembled at the high school. The spring before we had graduated from one or another of our town's four elementary schools, where we had stooped to water fountains and drawn time charts on brown paper. Now we watched with furtive interest while the juniors and seniors parked their cars with a single deft twist of the steering wheel. This was the grown-up world we had been waiting for, fervently and secretly, but once here most of us knew we had still a long way to travel. Our limbs were ungainly, ridiculous. We twitched in our seats; our elbows and knees, scratched and scabbed, behaved like children's. We knew we couldn't lounge at our lockers with the proper air of unconcern, nor did we suppose we could sit upright and motionless for the duration of the "Hallelujah Chorus" from Handel's *Messiah* or a Beethoven sonata. Yet under Miss Hughes's surveillance, we learned to do so. If the grind of a chair's legs or a sigh reached her ears, Miss Hughes carefully lifted the needle from the spinning record and, staring vaguely into space, showing no sign that she recognized the source of the disturbance, waited until the room was silent before beginning again.

In other classes we doodled in our notebooks, drawing caricatures of our teachers, words streaming from their mouths in balloons. Small pink erasers flew through the air. On the Monday morning following a stormy bout with us on Friday, Mrs. Trevelyan, our math teacher, was tearful. "My weekend was ruined," she told us. "It troubles me very much when we don't get along together. Surely we can do better, can't we? If we make a little effort?" We looked at her with stony eyes. To our social studies teacher, Miss Guthrie, we were deliberately cruel. Her voice was high, her mouth was tense, and often when she spoke a tiny thread of spittle hung between her lips. If someone answered a question in a strangled voice, mimicking her, she pretended not to notice.

Miss Hughes neither cajoled nor ignored us. Instead she made us her confidants. Music class met on Friday afternoons and through the windows the dusty autumn sunlight fell in long strips across our backs and onto the wooden floor. Behind us, flecked with high points of light, trees lined one end of the playing field. It was hard to tell, turning to look after a record had wound to its end, if the sun was striking to gold a cluster of leaves still green and summery or if a nighttime chill had done it.

The class always followed the same turn: first, Miss Hughes dictated to us what she called "background," pausing long enough for us to take down what she said in the notebooks we kept specially for her class, or for her to write on the blackboard a word we might not know how to spell. *To what class of stringed instruments does the pianoforte belong?* We wrote: *The pianoforte belongs to the dulcimer class of stringed instruments.* Or: *Name several forerunners of the pianoforte. Several forerunners of the pianoforte are the clavichord, the virginal, the harpsichord, the spinet.* If giggles rose involuntarily in our throats at the word "virginal," we managed to suppress them.

Following dictation, which she delivered without comment or explanation, she would ask us to assume our "postures." We had already written down the name of the piece we were about to hear, its composer, and usually some fact having to do with its performance—*on the harpsichord, the third movement of Mozart's Sonata in A Major, otherwise known as the "Turkish March," played by Wanda Landowska.* After she had set the needle on its course, we were for the moment alone with ourselves, a fact we were given to understand by the face wiped clean of all expression she held before us. We were then free to think of whatever we liked: a nightmare we had almost forgotten from the night before; a dog shaking water from its back, the drops flying everywhere like rain; a plan we had made with a friend for the weekend. Or we were free simply to watch the dust floating in the shafts of sunlight, to follow a path the sounds led us up and down.

We marveled that Miss Hughes always knew exactly when to turn and lift the needle, that she knew without looking when the record was almost over. After she had replaced the arm in its clasp, she turned her full attention to us. "You have just heard, boys and girls, in the 'Turkish March,' a great virtuoso performance. What do I mean by 'virtuoso'? A virtuoso performance is one executed by an instrumentalist highly skilled in the practice of his art, one who is able to bring to our ears music that we would otherwise go to our graves without hearing. The first great virtuosi pianists were Liszt and the incomparable Chopin, both of whom you will meet in due course.

"In fact, boys and girls," she said, lowering her voice a little so that we had to lean forward to hear, "we have our own virtuosi pianists, ones who regularly perform close by in New York City, only half an hour's ride away on the train from Pelham. You have heard the name Arthur Rubinstein, perhaps? You have heard the name Myra Hess? These are artists whose work you must do everything in your power to appreciate firsthand. We go to sleep at night, we wake in the morning, we blink twice and our lives are over. But what do we know if we do not attend?"

Miss Hughes suddenly held up her two hands in front of us, red fingernails flashing. "You will see, boys and girls, I have a fine breadth of palm. My fingers are not as long as they might be, but I am able to span more than an octave with ease. Perhaps you do not find that remarkable. But I assure you that for a woman a palm of this breadth is rare. I had once a great desire to become a concert pianist myself. A very great desire. And I had been admitted to study at Juilliard with a teacher of renown. A teacher, Carl Friedberg, who in his youth in Frankfurt had been the student of Clara Schumann. Who had heard Liszt interpret his own compositions. When I went for my audition, when I entered the room where the piano was waiting and Mr. Friedberg was sitting nearby, I was afraid. I do not hide that from you, boys and girls, I was very much afraid. But as soon as I began to play Chopin's Polonaise in A flat, a piece that requires much busy finger work by the left hand and a strong command of chords, I was so carried away by the fire of the music that I forgot the teacher. I forgot the audition. I forgot everything except the fact that I was now the servant of something larger than myself. When I reached the end and looked up—and I was in a bit of a daze, I may tell you—the great teacher's eyes were closed. He bowed his head once, very simply. That was all. I left the room. Soon afterward I received a letter assuring me that he would be proud to have me as his student."

Miss Hughes's face had registered the sweep of feelings she was recounting to us. Her eyes had narrowed with her great desire to be a pianist; entering the audition room, her jaw had grown rigid with fear; and while the great teacher had sat listening to her play, her face had assumed the look we were familiar with, the mask. Now her dark eyes took on a dreamy expression we had not yet seen. She seemed to be looking for words in a place that absorbed all her attention, over our heads, out the window, beyond.

"It was that winter, boys and girls, that my destiny revealed itself to me. Everything I had hoped for, worked for, practicing seven hours each day after I had finished giving lessons—everything was snatched away in a single instant. I will tell you how it happened. Because someday in your own lives you may wake to a new world in which you feel a stranger. And you will know, if by chance you remember our conversation here today, that someone—no, my dear boys and girls, many others, a host of others, have also risen to a dark morning.

"A friend, a friend whom I loved, had asked if I would accompany him on a skiing trip to Vermont. Of course I said yes. Why should I not? We were to spend a day on the slopes. I was a great skier—my father had taught me when I was a child—and I looked forward to this holiday with the greatest excitement. I had been working hard that winter, too hard. It may have been fatigue that in the end brought about my ruin. Because taking a turn that at any other time I might have managed with ease, my legs shot out from beneath me. I let go of my pole and put out my hand, as any good skier knows not to do. Instead of fracturing a leg or a hip, both of which I might easily have spared, I injured my left hand, breaking three fingers that never properly healed."

This time Miss Hughes raised her left hand alone. She must have been about to point out to us the fatally injured fingers when the bell rang and she immediately dropped her arm. "To each of you a pleasant weekend, boys and girls," she said, turning to replace her records in their sleeves.

By class the following Friday we had other things to think about, and perhaps she did as well. We had just listened to Bach's Fugue in G Minor, for the purpose of learning to recognize the sound of the oboe—and the room for once had an air not of enforced constraint but of calm—when Miss Hughes lifted her head and, looking out the window, told us that there was one of us, sitting now in our midst, who listened to music in a manner quite unlike the rest. "He listens as if for his life, boys and girls, and it is in this manner that the music of the anointed was written. For the composer, the sounds struggling in his imagination are a matter of life and death. They are as necessary to him as the air he breathes."

She kept us in no more suspense, but allowed her gaze to rest on a boy who always sat, no matter the classroom, at the end of a row. We had scarcely noticed him at all, those of us who had not gone to elementary school with him. But there he sat, at this moment, blushing. His hair was sandy, his face was freckled, and he wore glasses with clear, faintly pinkish rims. His name was Norman de Carteret, a name that in a room full of Daves and Mikes and Steves we found impossible to pronounce without lifting our eyebrows. During the first week of September, Miss Hughes had asked him how he would like us to say his last name, and he had answered quietly, so quietly we could scarcely hear him, that it was Carteret, pronouncing the last syllable as if it were the first letter of the alphabet. The "de" he swallowed entirely.

"Then," Miss Hughes had said, "your father or his father must have come from France, the country that gave us Rameau, that invaluable spirit who for the first time set down the rules of harmony. The country to which we are indebted as well for Debussy, who accomplished what might have been thought impossible: he permitted us to hear the sound of moonlight."

I knew something about Norman the others didn't. My mother had lived in our town as a child and occasionally met on the street someone she would later explain was once a friend of her mother's, dead long ago when my mother was sixteen. Hilda Kelleher was one of these friends, even a cousin of sorts, and lived in a large, brown-shingled Victorian house, not far from the station. A wide porch, in summer strewn with wicker rocking chairs, ran along the front and disappeared around one side. The other end of the house was flanked by tall pines that in winter received the snow. Hilda was of an uncertain age—older than my mother, but maybe not a full generation older. Her hair was dyed bright yellow, and when she smiled her mouth twitched up at one corner, uncovering teeth with traces of lipstick on them. Hilda had never married, but there was nothing strange in that. The town was full of old houses in which single women who had grown up in them lived on with their aging mothers, going "to business," teaching in the schools, supplementing their incomes in whatever ways they could. I supposed that they, too, had been girls, just as I was then, walking on summer nights beneath streetlights that threw leafy shadows on the sidewalks, that they, too, had listened to the murmur of voices drifting from screened porches, had heard the clatter of passing trains and dreamed of what would happen to them next. But life had passed them by, that was clear.

Hilda had dealt with the problem of dwindling resources by taking in boarders. An aunt of my mother's, a retired art teacher who, as my mother used to say, "had no one in the world," was looking for a place to live. One afternoon in late summer, just before school opened, my mother visited Hilda to inquire about arrangements and I went with her. While they sat talking in rocking chairs on the front porch, I discovered around to the side a swing hanging from four chains. It was easy to imagine sitting there on summer nights behind a screen of vines, morning glories closed to the full moon, listening to the cicadas. Swinging back and forth I could hear their voices, my mother's telling Hilda how Aunt Ruth had lived in Mrs. Hollingsworth's house in Tarrytown, how this arrangement would seem familiar to her. I heard Hilda saying how glad she was that a room was available, that we would look at it in a moment. She went on to say that one boarder, who had been with her a year, had moved out of the room into a smaller one that better suited his means. Did my mother know a Mr. de Carteret? He had a son who was going to the high school, she thought, in the fall. The son lived with the mother but came to visit the father on Saturdays. The terrible thing was that when he came the father wouldn't open the door of his room to him.

Her voice sank so low that I got out of the swing and crept along the wall to listen. "The poor child," she said in a loud whisper. "He knocks, and when his father won't let him in he sits outside the door in the hall. Saturday after Saturday he comes to the house and waits outside the room and still his father won't see him. Sometimes—oh, the poor child, I wish I knew what to do—he is there all afternoon."

Although I couldn't see her from where I was standing, I imagined my mother listening, her green eyes bright with sympathy, her rocking chair at rest. Her face would be quiet, reflective, as if her deepest convictions were being confirmed. "Everyone has some secret suffering," she'd say. "If we only knew."

I was back in the swing by the time they called me to look at the vacated room. We followed Hilda up a staircase of wide oak steps and along a hall, passing mahogany doors on either side. At last she threw one open on a room that had a neat bed covered with a white spread, a desk, and a chest of drawers. Pines stood in the window. My mother said she couldn't imagine that her aunt wouldn't be happy here; the room seemed to breathe tranquility. We closed the door, then went down the hallway to the staircase and out of the house.

I had been wondering whether or not I should whisper to my closest friends what I had heard Hilda say about Norman, but after Miss Hughes had asked us to notice his perfect attention, it seemed to me I should not. Why not, I couldn't be sure, except it seemed that if he were listening "as if for his life," he had heard something in the music that I hadn't, and I didn't think the others had either. I felt out of my depth. And soon enough, by saying nothing, by keeping to myself what I took to be his secret, I came to feel that some understanding had sprung up between us, that we shared a knowledge hidden from the others.

Then, very soon, our paths crossed.

II

In our old school there had been a classroom filled with books that we called the library. Twice a week we sat in a circle around Miss Kendall, the librarian, while she read to us, turning the book around from time to time to show us the pictures. I knew the books I wanted to read in that library; they were not the history books urged on us by our teachers, or the books about boys running away to sea, or even the large and lavishly illustrated volumes of myths and fairy tales. It was stories about girls I wanted, mostly orphan girls, or at least girls, like Sarah Crewe, whose mothers were dead and who had been left to the care of cruel adults to whom they refused to be grateful, to whom, in moments of passion, they poured out their long-suppressed feelings of outrage.

I had tried to explain all this to the older girl in the high school library who was supposed to show us around, and she had said I might like to read *Jane Eyre*, by Charlotte Brontë, pointing to shelves lodged in a corner. I should look under the *B*'s, she said, but I ended up nearby, facing shelves where all the books were written by people whose names began with a *C*. I was stopped by a title: *Lucy Gayheart*, a book about a girl, and perhaps even the kind I had in mind. It was written by

Willa Cather, a name I had never heard, and I quickly looked around for a place to read.

This library was much larger than our old one, and instead of a little table where books were set on their ends for display—picture books and books for older children with such titles as *The Story of Electricity* and *Abigail Adams: A Girl of Colonial Days*—here there were unadorned long tables stretching the width of the room, with chairs tucked in on either side. High windows filled one end, and beneath them the librarian sat at her desk, inkpad and rubber date stamps poised at her elbow. I had sat down and opened the dark blue cover of my book to the first page when I looked up and saw Norman de Carteret sitting across the table, poring over an immense open volume. One foot was drawn up to rest on the seat of his chair, and as he read he leaned his face against his knee. It was a book about ships, I could see that; there was a full-scale picture of a sloop, or a schooner, with all its sails unfurled. There was writing on the different parts of the ship and on the sails, too, probably to let you know what they were called. Norman was absorbed, and I began to read:

"In Haverford on the Platte the townspeople still talk of Lucy Gayheart. They do not talk of her a great deal, to be sure; life goes on and we live in the present. But when they do mention her name it is with a gentle glow in the face or the voice, a confidential glance that says: 'Yes, you, too, remember?' They still see her as a slight figure always in motion; dancing or skating, or walking swiftly with intense direction, like a bird flying home."

Lucy was one of the vivid creatures I wanted to read about, that was clear, but there was something that seemed not quite right, some note I had not yet heard. The story was already over and she lived on the first page not as a living person but as a memory.

I read on and to my surprise saw that Lucy, like Miss Hughes, wanted to be a pianist. She had been giving lessons to beginners from the time she was in tenth grade and had left Haverford to study music with a teacher in Chicago. Now she had come home for the Christmas holidays and had gone skating with her friends on the Platte. A young man, Harry, had joined them, and at sunset Lucy and he had sat together on a bleached cottonwood log, where the black willow thicket behind them made a screen. "The interlacing twigs threw off red light like incandescent wires, and the snow underneath was rose-color.... The round red sun was falling like a heavy weight; it touched the horizon line and sent quivering fans of red and gold over the wide country.... In an instant the light was gone.... Wherever one looked there was nothing but flat country and low hills, all violet and grey."

These words, too, seemed remarkable, because I thought I recognized the place. In our town, if you followed the railroad tracks over the bridge that looked down on Main Street, on past the redbrick factory and Catholic church, you came to a reservoir that in spring was overhung with Japanese cherry trees, their branches weeping pink blossoms into the black water. During the winter months, when the reservoir had frozen over, we skated there. No prairie surrounded the water, only rocks and frozen grass and crouching woods; but the sky loomed wide overhead, and on winter afternoons the red sun was caught for a moment in the drooping silver branches of the cherry trees. I thought I knew how the Platte would look, the sun going down on it, thought I knew how afterward everything would turn ordinary and flat.

Norman was still contemplating the picture of the sailing ship. I could glimpse him sitting there as I lowered my head to continue reading. Now Lucy and Harry were settled in a sleigh that was, I read, "a tiny moving spot on that still white country settling into shadow and silence. Suddenly Lucy started and struggled under the tight blankets. In the darkening sky she had seen the first star come out; it brought her heart into her throat. That point of silver light spoke to her like a signal, released another kind of life and feeling that did not belong here." I closed the book, deciding for today to forget *Jane Eyre*. I knew I had never read a book like this one. I had been expecting someone else to come along, or for Lucy and Harry to say something surprising or romantic to each other, something to happen besides the round red sun falling on the prairie and the star speaking to Lucy like a signal. And yet I felt that in this book these were enough. The pages I had read threw open the strange possibility that looking at things, feeling them, were also things that happened to you, just as much as meeting someone or going on a trip. What you thought and felt when you were alone or silently in the presence of someone else also made a story.

I looked up to see that Norman seemed to have fallen asleep on his book. His glasses were standing on their lenses beside him on the table and his face was in his arms. When the bell shrilled through the room, his shoulders twitched and he raised his head from the picture of the boat with all its sails. Looking up, still half asleep, his shortsighted blue eyes came to rest on mine. Another time I might have looked away. But as I, too, was half asleep, entertaining visions of quivering fans of red and gold playing on the prairie, turning over my new thoughts, I realized only after a moment that Norman had smiled at me as if he were still dreaming, as if he had been alone and, suddenly seized by a happy idea, were smiling at himself in a mirror.

❧

III

One Friday afternoon in October we filed into Miss Hughes's classroom to find her standing beside the day's album of records, dressed entirely in white. Her dress, made of soft white wool, fell just below her knees. There was no crimson or purple scarf tied round her neck; instead, a long necklace of pearls hung between her breasts.

"You will be wondering, boys and girls," she said to us as soon as we were seated, "why you find me today dressed as you see. I am in mourning, but a mourning turned to joy. White is the color of sorrow, as it is of radiance. And today I am going to play for you a piece of music that throughout your lives you will return to again and again. If ever you must make a decision, if ever you find yourselves tossing on a stormy sea—and life will not spare you, boys and girls; it spares no one—I beg you to do as I say. Find a spot where no living soul will disturb you, not even your dearest friend, and in the silent reaches of your soul listen to the music you are about to hear. Today we shall have no dictation, because it is my idea that Mozart's *Requiem* is best introduced without preliminaries. A requiem, you must know, is a prayer for the dead. Today we shall hear the opening section of this great work. One day— we shall see when—I shall play for you another."

Miss Hughes lowered the needle to the record that was already in place and spinning on the turntable. For a few moments a mournful sound filled the room, something that seemed to move forward, as if people were walking—a rhythmic, purposeful sound, with an echo for every step— when suddenly, without any warning, a blare of trumpets and kettle drums broke it all up, a frightening, violent blast that made us jump in our seats. Then, into the clamor, a chorus of men's voices forced their way, low, solemn, moving forward as before, but confident, as if they were sure of what they were saying. We were just getting used to the chorus when high above all the rest floated a single woman's voice, a voice raised high above the world but sliding down to meet it, and so calm, so full of understanding, I could have cried.

Miss Hughes lifted the needle and allowed her face to keep the expression of the mask for a few moments longer than usual. Then she drew a deep breath. "To comment on this music, boys and girls, would be an impertinence. We must let it rest in us where it will. *Rest*: a word, as it is used in music, to mean the absence of sound, a silence, sometimes short and sometimes long, when we hear only the vibrations of what has come before and prepare for those that will follow. You will understand what I mean if you think of a wave, the kind you see in a Japanese painting, caught in that moment just before it breaks."

The record had remained spinning on the turntable, its black surface crossed by a silver streak of light. Now Miss Hughes bent down, turned the knob, and the record slowly wound to a halt. Then she again stood upright, facing us. "The word *requiem*—a Latin word you of course already know—might best be translated by several words in English: may he find rest at last, the one who has died. But my own prayer, I shall tell you now, is that we, the living, may find rest within the span of our own lives. I mean that rest we know only when we are most awake to sorrow and to joy, when we find we can no longer tell the difference. Then we are living outside of time, as we are when we are listening to music such as that we have just heard. In such an instance, death is only something that happens to us, like being born or growing old, but is of less consequence than the many deaths we sustain in life. I mean the deaths, my friends, when our dearest hopes are blasted."

Miss Hughes had been speaking slowly, meditatively, choosing her words with care. Her eyes had gone from one of us to the other. Now she assumed the dreamy look we had seen once before. She looked beyond us, through the clear panes of the window, into the distance. "Because, boys and girls, death may come to us in many disguises. You see, I, too, have gone down into the waters.

"I think I have told you already that my great desire in life was to have become a pianist, to play for myself one of the late piano concerti of Chopin, let us say, or of Schubert's impromptus. To that end I was living in Paris, studying with a teacher who was drawing from me all those feelings that I had supposed—young as I was—must remain outside music, separate from it. I had embraced discipline, and practicing for hours and hours every day was the only way I knew to approach a sonata or prelude. It was this teacher who showed me that music is composed by a spirit alive to suffering and to joy and must be played by another such spirit. That it was only by bringing every moment of my life to the music that I could hope to draw from it what the composer had put in."

For a moment Miss Hughes seemed to wake from a sleep and looked at us alertly. "As indeed, boys and girls, in this room we must bring every moment of our lives to the music as we listen."

I wondered, while she stared from face to face, if her damaged hand had healed by the time she arrived in Paris, or if all this had taken place sometime before the skiing accident. But I would no more have thought to ask her than to ask whether or not Lucy Gayheart had taken the train back to Chicago, the night after she sat on the log and saw the red light fade from the prairie. The facts, the before and after of events, had their own logic by which, trusting the source, I supposed they must take their place in some pattern hidden from me.

Miss Hughes was playing with her pearls, winding them around her fingers. Again her gaze had retired to a place beyond the window.

"The city of light, boys and girls; that's what you will hear Paris called. But it is also, I will tell you, the city of darkness. If you cross the Pont des Arts one day, you will see the Île de la Cité, that great barge of an island, drifting up the river, the River Seine, I'm sure you know. And on that island, as you make your way across the bridge, you will see swing slowly into view a spectacle that has greeted the eyes of bewildered humanity for almost eight hundred years, the great square towers of Notre-Dame. I say 'slowly,' you will notice, because like the opening of the requiem we have just heard, like Bach's Fugue that stirred our souls a few weeks ago, that's how many of the best things come to us. The catastrophes stop us in our tracks. I know, my friends, because I came to a halt on the bridge that day; I was unable to continue my walk. I had a letter with me that I had only just received and that had thrown me into a state of the most painful confusion."

In the silence that followed these words we could hear the excited cawing of crows on the playing field behind us. "The letter was from a close friend at home relating the pitiable state into which my father had fallen. A debilitating illness from which he could not recover. The friend, who was old himself, did not ask me to return. But how could I think of anything else? Who would care for my father if I did not? I was all he had in the world, and it was to him that I owed my early life in music, he who had given me my first lessons on the piano. Of course I must return to look after him.

"And yet—and here, my dear boys and girls, I do not seek an answer—how would that be possible? To leave Paris, to leave the city in which I had been so happy! To leave all those feelings I had begun to put into my music! In short, to leave my teacher! It was not to be thought of. I leaned out over the edge of the bridge and looked down into the river flowing beneath. I could not see my way. I tasted the bitter waters of despair. Oh, I was tempted! Finally, scarcely knowing how I got there, I found myself in my room, and after closing the door and pulling the shutters, I listened to Mozart's *Requiem*. By the time it had concluded I knew my way."

Miss Hughes, standing immobile in white, continued to gaze out the window. Surely the class would be over in a minute or two, but she didn't seem to recollect our presence. I stealthily turned my head to see sleek black crows lifting out of the trees and lighting back into them, their outspread wings glinting in the afternoon light, the branches with all their yellow leaves tossing up and down.

IV

In the days that followed, I decided that Miss Hughes had been in love with her teacher. She must have been, I thought, because I had now followed Lucy Gayheart to Chicago where she lived alone in a room at the top of a stairs. A room, perhaps, like the room in Paris to which Miss Hughes had stumbled and had drawn shutters on a bright day. Lucy Gayheart was not in love with her teacher, but her teacher had urged her to attend a concert given by a celebrated singer named Clement Sebastian who, although he lived in France, was spending the winter in Chicago. "Yes, a great artist should look like that," she had thought the moment he had walked onto the stage. And then he had sung a Schubert song.

The song was sung as a religious observance in the classical spirit, a rite more than a prayer: "*In your light I stand without fear, O august stars! I salute your eternity.* . . . Lucy had never heard anything sung with such elevation of style. In its calmness and serenity there was a kind of large enlightenment, like daybreak."

I remembered that Lucy had struggled up in Harry's sleigh when she had seen the first star flashing to her on the wide prairie, and I thought perhaps this was what Miss Hughes had meant about listening for your life: what you heard in the music was something exalted that you already knew, but weren't aware that you did, something you had blindly felt or heard or seen.

But then, reading on, I learned that Lucy's mood had quickly changed. There was to be no more serenity and calm. "She listened to Sebastian sing five more Schubert songs, all of them melancholy, and felt that there was something profoundly tragic about this man. . . . She was struggling with something she had never felt before. A new conception of art? It came closer than that. A new kind of personality? But it was much more. It was a discovery about life, a revelation of love as a tragic force, not a melting mood, of passion that drowns like black water."

Although I didn't understand exactly how the music had led to this discovery, I knew that in this book, called by her name, I was not reading about Lucy alone. The lines that came next made it clear she was merely one member of a select company, a company set apart—as Miss Hughes had set Norman apart—by a destiny determined from within: "Some people's lives are affected by what happens to their person or their property; but for others fate is what happens to their feelings and their thoughts—that and nothing more."

V

One Saturday afternoon in late October my mother asked if I would take Hilda and Aunt Ruth a lemon poppy-seed cake she had made for them. It was not only Aunt Ruth she felt had no one in the world, but Hilda as well. "Poor souls," she had said. "To be all alone like that." I put the cake, wrapped in wax paper, in the straw basket that hung from the handlebars of my bike. The leaves were now almost gone from the trees, but the day was clear and warm, like a day in early September. In less than a week it would be Halloween, and although we now thought it childish to go out begging, it was nice to think about walking from house to house, the night with its bare branches stark against a sky filled with spirits riding the air. I was in no rush to arrive at Hilda's because Aunt Ruth made me uneasy. When she came to our house she would give paper and colored pencils to my younger sisters and me and instruct us to let our imaginations run wild. Our older brother Charlie would already have walked away. He might be roaming outside with his friends, climbing rocks, or riding his bike around the streets. As a boy, he would not have been expected to look after the lonely ones our mother invited. Nor would our father, who continued to read his book undisturbed in another room. After a few minutes Aunt Ruth would inspect our efforts and to mine she would say, "D minus." Just as she might say the same if one of us carried her a cup of coffee that was not hot enough. But how could you obey a direction to let your imagination run wild? It was like someone wishing you sweet dreams.

By the time Hilda's house came into view, I was riding my bike in loops, swerving sharply toward one curb then the other, doubling back. In the middle of the street I made a circle, three times. I knew now it was not so much Aunt Ruth I was afraid of running into; it was Norman de Carteret. Suppose he was sitting in the dark hall outside his father's door? Or suppose I met him coming out of the house as I was going in?

And then, my bike making wider and wider loops both toward and away, going over in my mind what I would say to Norman if we happened to meet, I finally dared to look up and saw him there on the porch at the side of the house, sitting on the swing that hung from four chains. The morning-glory vines were bare, and he was sitting with his feet against the porch railing, pushing himself back and forth. I could see, too, that when he saw me he flinched and lowered his head to hide his face. But then, as I was about to ride by, pretending I hadn't seen him, he looked up and—as he had done in the library—smiled. I parked my bike at the bottom of the steps, removed the cake from the basket, and went around the corner of the porch to where he was sitting.

"Hi," he said. His brown high-top sneakers were resting on the porch railing. Behind his glasses his blue eyes floated a little.

"Hi," I said. There was a long pause before I thought of something to say. "My aunt lives here."

"I know." His voice was high and childish. "So does my father."

I sat down on the railing not far from his feet, swung my legs up, and leaned back against one of the round white pillars. It seemed surprising that Norman spoke of his father. Had he knocked on his door this morning and, like all the other times, been greeted with silence? Had he been waiting in the hall for hours, not knowing what to do, and finally come down to sit on the swing?

"Did you come here to see him?" I asked, both fearful and eager that he say more.

"Yes," he answered, looking straight ahead, out between the vines that in August had made a screen from the sun. Now a few shriveled leaves hung in the warm afternoon. Just as at school, Norman was wearing corduroy trousers a little too big for him, and a plaid flannel shirt buttoned at the neck. The sleeves came down almost to his knuckles. "I'm waiting till he wakes up. He told me not to go away. He wants me to wait for him here."

"Oh," I said and came to a stop. His voice had something in it I thought I recognized. It was in Miss Hughes's voice when she stared out the window while the crows were squawking and flapping in the trees. But Miss Hughes, as she stood there with her hands clasped at her waist, seemed to be communing with something only she could see. Norman's face, on the other hand, had lost its dreamy quality: his freckles stood out while he spoke; his eyes looked sharp and aware. He was looking at me as if he had made a point that he expected me to respond to.

Suddenly overcome with anxiety, not knowing what to answer, wanting only to erase the look in his eyes that made me afraid, I started unwrapping the cake. "Want some?" I asked.

"Sure," he said, and when I broke off a large chunk and held it out to him, he leaned forward in the swing and took it in a hand I could see was trembling. I broke off another chunk for myself. At first we ate demurely, silently, spilling a few crumbs around us and brushing them away. I would find a way later on, I thought, to explain to my mother about the cake. I knew after she'd heard the story—even if annoyed at first—she would be pained. I swallowed a piece that was too big for me and choked and sputtered, and then, on purpose this time, crammed a fistful in my mouth, pretending to frown at him disapprovingly, as if he were the one stuffing his mouth, until suddenly I was aping convulsions, bent double, holding my side, almost falling off the railing. Norman at first looked on, snorting with laughter. Then he, too, snatched a handful of cake and shoved it in his mouth, and soon we were both grabbing for more, exploding in high giggles, looking at each other cross-eyed, holding our sides, pretending to be on the point of collapse, pretending to be falling and dying, until the cake had disappeared, lying around us in half-eaten pieces.

Gradually we subsided, our shoulders stopped shaking, and we could breathe without gasping for air. The afternoon grew quiet around us. We could hear children playing up the block and the sound of someone raking leaves. Inside the house someone began to play the piano, some song from a time before we were born, something the grown-ups had sung when they were young. On the other side of the hedge, the late sun struck a large window into a flaming pool of orange. We avoided each other's eyes as if we had shared a secret we were ashamed of. After a while whoever was playing the piano broke off abruptly in the middle of a song—as if fed up with the wrong notes that kept interrupting the melody surging just behind—and closed the cover with a bang. The sun slipped from the window, the branches of the trees reached ragged above our heads. When I finally got to my feet, taking leave of Norman without saying a word, it was almost dark.

For a few days afterward I tried falling in love with Norman de Carteret. I passed him in the halls sometimes, and once caught sight of him at his locker, turning his combination lock. But since our afternoon on Hilda's porch, we were shy with each other, lowering our eyes when we met. Once, in music class, when Miss Hughes was playing a Brahms quintet for clarinet and strings, I tried to imagine how he might be listening, perhaps in the way Lucy had listened to Sebastian sing the Schubert songs. He was seated behind me, at the end of the row, and when I turned my head very slightly I could see him sitting there, his eyes sharp and aware, as they had been when he talked about his father. But at the end of the class when he walked through the door, his corduroy pants hanging from his hips, I could see he was only a child like myself.

During the following weeks I pursued the story of Lucy Gayheart in fits and starts. I read with a sense of exaltation and impending doom, dipping back from time to time, for reassurance, into the world of Sara Crewe and Anne of Green Gables. There was some new strain in the voice telling the story, something I had not encountered in any other book. It ran along beneath the words like a stream beneath a smooth surface of ice, some undertone murmuring, "This is the way life is, this is the way life is." It was a voice—dispassionate, stern—I listened for with joy, as if it brought news from a country for which I had long been homesick. And yet my nightly dreams told me, too, it was a country where terror and brutality might strike out of a benign blue sky. It seemed not so much that my child life was fading into the past. It was more that my entire future life was rising before me, as if it were already known to me, as if it had already happened long ago and was waiting to be remembered.

Despite my fitful reading, Lucy's story was quickly running its course. She had already become Clement Sebastian's piano accompanist, already fallen in love with him. He was Europe, the wide world, the brave life of feelings, unabashed and unashamed, not cramped or peevish as in Haverford. He was a singer, an artist. And although he was married, he had fallen in love with Lucy, with her youth, her enthusiasm, perhaps with her rapturous admiration of himself, he who was disillusioned and tired of the world. And so when Harry came to see her in Chicago, to take her to a week of operas and to propose marriage, she told him desperately that she couldn't marry him, that she was in love with someone else.

None of this seemed surprising. The undertone I listened for, I knew, had something to do with desire, with wanting someone who wasn't there. Or maybe someone who was there but whom you couldn't reach out and touch. It had to do with feelings that couldn't be spoken and yet had to be spoken, the space between.

But now Lucy's story was taking an unexpected turn, was moving in directions my daytime self would not have thought possible. In response to what Lucy told him, Harry, in a fit of pique, married a woman lacking in that quick responsiveness he had loved in Lucy, and regretted the marriage immediately. Sebastian left Chicago for a summer concert tour in Europe and met a sudden death. In despair, Lucy returned to Haverford, to a "long blue-and-gold autumn in the Platte valley."

Then January came and "the town and all the country round were the color of cement." Lucy left the house one afternoon to skate on the river, just as we would soon be skating on our reservoir with its weeping trees. What she didn't know was that the bed had shifted, that what once had been only a narrow arm of the river had become the swift-flowing river itself. She skated straight out onto the ice, large cracks spreading all around her. For a moment she was waist deep in icy water, her arms resting on a block of ice. Then "the ice cake slipped from under her arms and let her down."

I was incredulous. Despite the opening sentences of the book, I thought I hadn't understood and read the passage over and over, looking for some hint, some odd word or phrase, that would change its meaning. And yet, even while searching, even while trying to reassure myself that I must have missed something, I was aware—by some inner quaking that echoed the sound of splintering ice—I had understood very well. Harry is left to take up a life racked with remorse that only time will soften, and Lucy slips into the regions of the remembered. It was as the undertone running beneath the story had assured all along: Lucy's response to Sebastian's songs, her bleak sense of foreboding, would be fulfilled. An early death—anticipated by the intense life of feelings—had been her destiny, and at the appointed time her death had risen to meet her. This, I supposed, was what people called tragedy.

VI

Because of Haverford, whose sidewalks Lucy had walked in the long autumn of her return, the houses and streets of our town looked different, the late gardens of chrysanthemums and Michaelmas daisies, the silver moon rising above them. In the November afternoons we ran up and down the hockey field in back of the school, and even at four o'clock the red bayberries flickered in the twilight. Walking home, thinking of Lucy, I noticed the cracks in the sidewalks, the way the roots of trees had splintered them. Beneath the sidewalks ran a river of fast-flowing roots that could throw slabs of cement into the air, make a graveyard of the smooth planes where we used to roller-skate and sit playing jacks. From the end of one street I could see the train station, its roof black against the orange sky, and could imagine the tracks running over the bridge and past the reservoir into the city. Even now Myra Hess might be practicing the Chopin she would play tonight to a crowd at Carnegie Hall. Perhaps Miss Hughes was sitting on the train that would take her to the concert; perhaps she would return late at night to a room in a big house like Hilda's, a room that looked out on pines.

For Thanksgiving my mother invited Hilda and Aunt Ruth, who must not be left alone. Hilda's lipstick, a wan hope, had left traces on her teeth, I took note, as she leaned across the table to ask if I had met Norman de Carteret in any of my classes. Before answering I vowed I would not, cost what it might, be trapped as she had been, would not become an old woman in a town where life was one long wait. Hilda went on to recount to the table at large that Mr. de Carteret, who had scarcely stirred from his room for months, had been busy during the last days buying a turkey to cook for his son. He had bought cranberry sauce and sweet potatoes, she told us, and a bag of walnuts. It was all assembled on the table in the kitchen, and she herself had contributed two bottles of ginger ale. She had helped him put the turkey in the oven several hours before and at this moment it must almost be done. She hoped he wouldn't leave it in so long that it dried out. She hoped, too, that he remembered to turn off the oven once he took it out, because something might catch fire. She wondered if she should telephone him now to warn him but was persuaded by my father that a fire was unlikely.

On Monday we were back in school. I didn't see Norman that day, or the next, or the next, not until Friday, when, passing in the hall, I caught sight of him standing at his locker. He was standing idly there, staring into it in his usual absent-minded way, not looking for anything in particular, it seemed. That was in the morning. By lunch a rumor had run through the school like fire through dry grass. One friend whispered it, and then another. Had I heard? Norman de Carteret's father had killed himself. Yes, it was true. He had drowned himself in the reservoir on Saturday. He'd done it by putting stones in his pockets. Someone's father had been part of the group that had pulled him from the water on Saturday night. That's why Norman hadn't been in school. All the teachers had been sent a notice, but Norman was in school today. Had I seen him? I had. What did he look like? Was he crying?

I absorbed the news as if it were of someone I knew nothing about, someone I had to strain to place or remember, someone whose name I barely recognized. Norman had again become a stranger, someone wrapped in an appalling story. My exchanges with him had separated me from the group; for a while I had shared his isolation and in drawing near him had drawn closer to my dreaming self, my reading self. Across from each other at the table in the library we had unreservedly lost ourselves in the pages of a book. Had greeted each other in our solitudes. And together on Hilda's porch we had become antic children playing for their lives, had watched those children dissolve in the waning afternoon. Together we had arrived at a threshold.

Now I wanted nothing more to do with him. I was terrified that recalling our shared silences might draw me into some vortex of catastrophe. My fear was akin to what I had felt when, reaching the end of Lucy's story, I had looked frantically for something to tell me that I had not understood, that the words printed so boldly in black on the white page spelled out a meaning I had not grasped. But in turning my back on Norman, I sensed that I was opening a door on some new loneliness inside myself. Shame waited just beyond the edge of fear. And a dawning realization that in denying Norman I was denying my own most secret yearnings, whatever it was Miss Hughes had recognized in him and that I wanted too. He would cross into some new place and I would be left behind, inconsolable.

All day there had been the promise of snow in the air, and when we filed into Miss Hughes's room a few stray flakes had begun to fall. They were there in the window, the first of the season. Norman was already sitting in his place at the end of a row and the snow was falling behind him. He was sitting bolt upright in his seat, staring straight ahead, the corners of his mouth twisted up into something like a grin. But we only glanced at him, we didn't stare, sitting down as quickly as we could in our own places to get him out of our sight. We were overwhelmed with curiosity but also repelled. It would have been better if he hadn't been there at all, if we could have gone over the story, embellishing it with each retelling, without having to look at him, without having to sit with him in the same room.

Miss Hughes was, as usual, standing in her place beside the phonograph, the album on the table beside her. She was wearing a dark gray dress with a scarf that shimmered blue one moment, green the next. We had not met for two weeks because of the Thanksgiving vacation, but she had told us the last time we had seen her that she would welcome us back by introducing us to that consummate artist, Chopin. Now, rather brusquely, without the preliminary remarks with which she usually asked us "to silently invite our souls in order to prepare for the journey ahead," she asked us to open our notebooks and she began to dictate. "For Chopin," she pronounced, "the keyboard was a lyric instrument. He told his students, 'Everything must be made to sing.'"

For a few moments there were the sounds of papers rustling and of pencil cases coming unzipped. Then we settled to writing down her words.

"Chopin was a romantic in his impulse to render passing moods, but he was a classicist in his search for purity of form. His work is not given to digression. The Preludes are visionary sketches, none of them longer than a page or two. 'In each piece,' Schumann said, 'we find in his own hand, "Frederic

Chopin wrote it!" He is the boldest, the proudest poet of his time.'"

We wrote laboriously, stopping as Miss Hughes carefully wrote on the board the words "classicist," "digression," "visionary." She made sure we had written quotation marks around Schumann's words, the exclamation point where it belonged. Out of the corner of my eye I saw that Norman was hunched over his notebook, writing.

Miss Hughes had turned to the album. "Now, boys and girls, we shall listen to one of Chopin's Preludes, the fourth, in E minor. It is very brief."

She drew a record out of its sleeve and placed it on the spinning turntable. After three months' training, we knew to assume our postures, so she had only to glance quickly around the room before lowering the needle. We heard the chords, the chords going deeper and deeper, and I pictured pine trees pointing to the sky at sunset; a darkness was about to overwhelm them, but for the moment they were lit by the setting sun. Everything was disappearing, the chords were telling us; a deep shadow was falling over the side of the mountain, yet the melody was singing of the last golden light thrown up from behind the rim.

"Do you hear it, boys and girls?" Miss Hughes asked us as she lifted the needle from the record. "Do you hear there the voice of desire? Not for one thing or another, not for a person or a place, but desire detached from any object. What we have heard in this fourth Prelude is the voice of longing when it breaks through into the regions of poetry, into the regions of whatever lives closest to us and furthest away."

Miss Hughes's scarf flashed blue then green against her gray dress, against the dark square of the blackboard behind her. Her eyes assumed the dreamy look we had seen before. "It was for this I had hopes of becoming a pianist," she told us, looking out the window. "To coax that voice from the instrument, to allow others to hear it in the way that I did." She was gazing into the snowflakes, it seemed, into the bare, black tree branches through which they were falling in the waning afternoon. She was watching them spill from the gray sky; in a trance she was following their white tumble. But all at once, as if she, too, were falling from some high place, as if she, too, were whirling through deep silent spaces, she seemed to catch herself. I had turned in my seat to look at the snow but also to catch a glimpse of Norman. He was sitting now with his face buried in his arms, as he had sat that day in the library.

Miss Hughes looked around her sleepily, and for the first time we saw her face, without the prompting of music, assume the mask. For a long moment she stood before us, impassive, mouth pulled down at the corners, eyes closed. When she opened them, they rested darkly on Norman's lowered head. She allowed them to remain there a few seconds, taking her time, as if she were inviting us to consider with her which words she might choose.

"Is there anything we can do for you, Norman?" she asked at last.

There was silence in the room. I thought of the snow hitting the ground and wondered whether it had already begun to cover the brown grass beneath the trees, of Norman's father lying somewhere in the earth, his body in its coffin perhaps already beginning to rot, his grave still raw and exposed. The snow would hide all that, the dirt piled on top, and if Norman went to look where his father was, he would see an even cover of white.

"Because," Miss Hughes continued, "we would like you to know that you are sitting in the company of friends."

She brooded, frowning, while we sat rigidly in our seats.

Then she turned her eyes from Norman to us. "You are perhaps not aware, boys and girls, that Mozart was Chopin's favorite composer. I shall now tell you a story. When Chopin died at the age of thirty-nine, in Paris, his funeral was held at the Madeleine, a church of that city. Afterward he was buried in a cemetery called *Père-Lachaise*, where you may someday wish to visit his grave. But at his funeral, it was Mozart's *Requiem* that the gathered mourners were given to hear. I once told you that before long we would listen together to another section of it. Today we shall hear the 'Lacrimosa.' The word means 'full of tears.'"

We waited while she returned the record we had heard to its sleeve and drew out another. She brooded over us now as a moment ago she had brooded over Norman. "We cannot see into the mysteries of another person's life, dear boys and girls. We have no way of knowing what deaths a soul has sustained before the final one. It is for this reason that we must never presume to judge or to speak in careless ways about lives of which we understand nothing. I tell you this so that you may not forget it. We may honor many things in life. But for someone else's sorrow we must reserve our deepest bow."

Miss Hughes had placed the record on the turntable and now paused before lowering the needle. "You will hear in the music that I am about to play for you a prayer for the dead, a prayer that they may at last find the peace that so often escapes us in life. Because, boys and girls, in praying for the dead, we are praying for ourselves in that hour when we, too, far away as that hour might seem to us now, shall join their ranks. But even more—and you will understand me in time—we are honoring the suffering in our own lives, those of us who barely know how we shall survive the day. If you listen closely, I know you cannot fail to hear something else: the tale of how our grief, the desire for what we do not have, the desire for what is forever denied us, may at length—when embraced as our destiny—become indistinguishable from our joy. Indistinguishable, you will understand, my dear friends, in that moment when time, as in the most sublime music, has ceased to be.

"When the record comes to an end I ask that you gather your things and silently take your leave. I shall look forward, in a week's time, to the return of your company."

We heard strings draw out one note and then two more, a little higher, the same pattern repeated three times, very sweet, very light, as if we might all float on these blithe strains forever. Into this—not denying but blending—broke a chorus of plaintive voices repeating something twice, voices asking, imploring, like a wind that moans in the night; then quickly gaining strength and conviction, they began an ascent, a climb, in which they mounted higher and higher, at each step becoming bolder, a procession like the first section we had heard weeks before. But now the voices surged as if straining toward something nobody had ever reached, up and up, the procession climbing higher and higher, the kettle drums pounding, the trumpets blaring, the echo falling in the wake of each step, until they could mount no higher and then— with utter simplicity, with utter calm—the voices returned to the point from which they had begun and pronounced their words in an ordinary manner, foot to earth.

When the record had spun to its end, when there was nothing more to listen for, we slowly picked up our books and filed out of the room. At the door I turned to look back and saw Miss Hughes still standing at attention before the phonograph, her hands together in front of her. Norman had not moved; his face was hidden in his arms. It was early December and already the room was filling with shadows, but the snow swirling at the window cast a restless light, the flickering light of water, over Miss Hughes's frozen mask, over Norman bowed at his desk. For the moment Miss Hughes was standing watch. But soon Norman would raise from his arms the face we had not yet seen and that would be his until, in life or in death, he opened his eyes on eternity.

Things Fall Apart

———

In memory of Chinua Achebe, 1930–2013

*The world is like a Mask, dancing. If you want to see
it well you do not stand in one place.*
—Chinua Achebe

I

I had been married only a few months when we went to live in Nigeria, a country that had become independent a short time before. It was September 1963, and the British presence in Nigeria was still strong. Half the staff at Igbobi College, where we taught were English, half were Nigerian; we were the sole Americans. We'd been told before arriving that the staff would include a family from Wales, but we didn't make sharp distinctions. We were both twenty-three, and neither of us had ever lived outside the United States nor done any traveling to speak of. Nonetheless, we had ideas.

We'd been sent by a small program called Teachers for West Africa, funded by Hershey Chocolate, whose cocoa supply came largely from Nigeria and Ghana. The situation in Ghana with a newly elected Nkrumah was considered volatile by our State Department, so we'd been sent to Nigeria, to Lagos, off the Gulf of Guinea on the Bight of Benin. We were avoiding the Peace Corps because we feared, with conflict brewing in Vietnam, it might be tainted by some strain of overheated patriotism. In fact, we knew nothing at

all about the Peace Corps. Nor, despite what we'd been told
of Hershey's philanthropic intentions, had we entered into
the sentiments of friends who'd praised us, as we prepared
to leave, for the humanitarian work it was assumed we'd
be undertaking. We hadn't seen it that way, felt vaguely
condescending toward those who spoke approvingly of our
desire "to help." We considered this the corrupted language
of colonialism. Indeed, it had been pleasant to tell people
we were going to Africa and observe their look of surprise.
Our own purposes, we thought, were admirably simple. We
wanted to travel the world, that was all. We would receive
scant pay and when we left Nigeria would take nothing with
us except a sharply enriched inner life.

We had as well a somewhat exalted sense that of course
Nigerians would feel easier with us than with the British,
whose formality, as we imagined it, would recall the oppressions
of Empire. We would be loved because we were Americans.
I had grown up just outside New York City. C. came from
the mountains of West Virginia. But these differences were
nothing: it was our nationality that mattered. Our common
culture's more relaxed social manners, distinct from what we
imagined to be the rigid observances of the British, would
allow Africans to feel at home with us. Of course we knew
nothing about African formalities of any kind but believed
that as Americans we didn't stand on ceremony. Without quite
saying so, we considered British manners the expression of a
class system that in Africa must take the form of racism, a way
of preserving distance between colonial masters and those they
exploited. We had little notion of what we meant by manners.
Nonetheless, we obscurely felt that with a more informal way
of approaching people we'd put them at their ease and at the
same time prove our own virtue.

These convictions were for the most part unarticulated. If they were riddled with contradictions, we saw nothing of that. Nor of the bland assumptions of our own right-thinking that fed them.

We arrived in Lagos at the very end of August to be in time for the new term, and our principal, Mr. Olatunbosun, was there to meet us at the airport in Ikeja. Climbing down from the plane, we were astonished, despite the intense midafternoon heat, to see Mr. Olatunbosun wearing a navy blue woolen jacket and tie. He welcomed us gravely, shook our hands, and asked if we were very tired after our long flight from London. Then he led us to his blue Peugeot 403, waiting just beyond. The driver helped put our bags into the trunk, or the "boot," as he called it, then held open one of the back doors for us and we climbed in, C. folding his long legs into the backseat. Mr. Olatunbosun got in beside the driver in the front seat, and over his shoulder made conversation as we drove down the Ikorodu road on our way to Yaba, where the school was located. Through a back window each of us stared out at a world in full swing: women in bright wrappers, green, gold, purple, carrying babies on their backs, schoolboys walking by the side of the road, some holding hands, little roadside stands with cardboard roofs. A tall boy lightly carried a sewing machine on his head, another carried a mattress. I reached for C.'s hand but let go after a minute, because of the heat. Before long we turned onto a road pocked by steep dips and mounds, and the Peugeot rocked up and down and finally passed through the gate of Igbobi College.

Bringing the car to a stop in the scant shade of a tree hung with grapefruits, the driver called out for someone to help; two barefoot boys in khaki shorts appeared and hauled our bags out of the car. We followed Mr. Olatunbosun along a path where a little goat with nubby horns nibbled the grass. Then we were seated in his office, which occupied a room piled high with papers on the ground floor of a shuttered house. A ceiling fan turned briskly above. Our principal looked at us through horn-rimmed glasses, the lenses a little smudged, and again bade us welcome. At forty, perhaps, he was not at all an old man but had a slow, deliberate manner. A boy entered balancing a tray on his shoulder, deposited it deftly on the large desk. We were served steaming cups of tea and what looked like Nabisco crackers. We'd been told repeatedly we must drink only water that had been boiled when we arrived in Africa, but a glance between us decided the question: politeness forbade our asking if the water was only very hot or had been brought to a boil. Our faces like Mr. Olatunbosun's were already running with sweat. We nibbled at the crackers. A large green lizard with an orange head and tail wriggled in at the door and then, as if stopped by the sight of us, froze in place.

We would be lodged, Mr. Olatunbosun explained, on the other end of the house where we were now sitting. He and his family lived in one half of the house and we would occupy the other: two rooms upstairs, two rooms down. An enormous avocado tree stood just beyond the open door, its shiny leaves already falling into the shadows of late afternoon. Ripe green fruit lay scattered in the sand beneath. Mr. Olatunbosun took from the bottom drawer of his desk two pieces of paper, handed one to each of us. These were our schedules, he told us, pronouncing the word as if it began with a "sh." We would be teaching English language and literature to the youngest boys, the ones in first form, who were about twelve years old, as well as to the oldest, those in upper sixth form, who would be sitting for their higher school certificates, exams set and marked in Cambridge, England. Each of the three terms was followed by a month's holiday, during which time we were free to travel or do as we liked. But when classes were in session we'd also be expected to take a turn supervising the students' noon and evening meals in the refectory.

We already knew that the school had been founded jointly by the Methodist Church and the Anglican Church, so we weren't surprised to learn that the day began with prayer. Although the students would include Hausa Muslims from the north, Mr. Olatunbosun explained to us, and others from Muslim families here in the south, no one was exempt from attending chapel. In fact, we'd find among our students—about two hundred in all—boys from all over Nigeria, some from the eastern part of the country, Igbos, and then many from Lagos itself, who mostly spoke Yoruba. Some of these last, of course, were day scholars. In response to C.'s question about the languages of Nigeria, Mr. Olatunbosun answered briefly that they were too numerous to name; we would slowly get an idea of some of them. Time would allow us to learn all we cared to know.

Our hour in his office hadn't seemed long but already dusk had fallen; in fact it was rapidly getting dark. A face appeared in the doorway and Mr. Olatunbosun slowly stood up and introduced us to Michael Bowen, the geography master, who would show us our rooms in the adjoining part of the house. We must be very tired, our principal said. And once again shaking hands with each of us, he said he hoped we'd rest well.

Michael told us, as soon as we'd turned away from the door of the principal's office and into the twilight, that he'd been chosen to show us around because it was thought that as Americans we'd find ourselves more at ease with him, someone from Wales.

"I'll do my best," he said, smiling on one side of his mouth.

Michael's dark hair rose in a crest above his forehead; he wore white blousy shorts and a white short-sleeved shirt. He said that as Europeans—a term we quickly learned was used for anyone whose ancestors had originated in Europe, whatever part of the globe they came from—we would find the heat difficult to cope with and would need someone to help us: a "steward," in this case someone who came with the house, who had been employed by its most recent occupants. We stepped across a tin-roofed causeway that led to a little structure apart, which Michael told us was the kitchen.

Then he ducked his head into a doorway of the house itself and flicked a switch. A light came on and an overhead fan whirred slowly into motion. A little white gecko, black eyes staring, wriggled away in one corner of the ceiling. It was clear we were in the dining room: a heavy wooden table and chairs stood in the middle, a sideboard against the wall. The steel shutters of the windows were closed to the night but a brown moth the size of a tiny bird flew in at the door.

Michael called out and Ben, a small barefooted man about the age of our parents, stepped into the room. He had deep markings up and down the sides of his face: tribal markings we learned to call them. Michael shook a cigarette out of the pack in his shirt pocket and wheeled around toward Ben. "Where's the match?"

Ben scrambled in a drawer of the sideboard.

"You'll be sacked if you're not there when you're wanted," Michael told him. He turned very slightly toward us and winked. My gaze fell on the smooth cement floor painted a deep brick red, on Ben's bare feet standing there, his cracked soles, his ragged toenails.

After Michael left us, I asked Ben if he had put the jar of green and red crotons in the center of the table. "For welcome," he said.

C. flicked off the ceiling bulb to discourage moths and we stood with Ben just outside the house, looking into the garden. The night was very black, tiny points of green light flashing everywhere, the air heavy with fireflies, each making its way alone in the great company. We didn't speak for a time, listened to the deafening clamor of night creatures. The racket was familiar from our own summer nights but now the volume seemed to have been turned way up. Did he live nearby, C. asked. Ben answered yes, along with his family, in the stewards' quarters. He went on to tell us there were snails in the garden and that he would prepare them for us to eat. He'd been a cook on the Elder Dempster line and had traveled everywhere: England, Scotland, France. He could prepare anything we liked. Steak and kidney pie. Trifle. Fish and chips. He looked at us as from across a distance.

We became aware mosquitoes were biting our ankles and soon followed Ben up a staircase that seemed to be all on the outside of the house, steps leading straight up to a wide landing where they doubled back and climbed to an upper porch, a verandah. There, behind a railing, a canvas sling-backed chair faced into the night.

But it wasn't until the next day—hours after we'd been woken by a sudden flash that illuminated the empty wardrobe in the corner with its doors standing open, a splintering crack followed by a roll of wet thunder that began at one corner of the sky and slowly made its way to the other—that I was able to see in the washed light of morning the staircase we'd climbed the night before. Could properly take in the wooden steps, painted light gray, a corrugated roof hanging above them to protect from rain or sun, could slowly go up and down marveling at the tender green vine that leapt from rung to rung, its pale purple trumpet flowers still holding last night's rain, its delicate new tendrils like the horns of a snail groping blindly in thin air.

II

During the coming days we were taken to the market to buy crockery, pots and pans, a metal pail for laundry; we soon learned to recognize the clink of the handle against the rim when Ben was washing our clothes. Bought a filter for purifying water, engaged a carpenter to make a screen door for the upstairs rooms. We learned to know pounds and pence and guineas, to call a shilling a bob. At Leventis, the Lebanese store where as in the market you could bargain, we bought a length of cloth to hang between the upstairs bedroom and sitting room. And at Kingsway, where you could not, we lavishly purchased an imported glass blue bowl where daily Ben arranged cuttings from the garden: golden allamanda, frangipani that gave off a heavy sweet scent.

In the streets of Lagos we encountered children with distended stomachs and those we learned to call lepers, saw blind people with staring sockets, beggars moving along with the help of a crutch. Grew accustomed to the sight of Ben ironing our clothes on a wooden board set up in the kitchen, or on his knees applying Mansion wax with a halved coconut to the dark mahogany boards of the sitting room floor, his back running with sweat.

Our guide, Michael, disappeared for unexplained reasons, but in the days just before the students returned from their holiday we were shown around the school by other teachers, or "masters," as they were called. One afternoon when Roy Jenkins, who taught chemistry at Igbobi, was taking us through the new labs, showing us the gleaming sinks and up-to-date Bunsen burners, he stopped midstream in his demonstrations, looked at me thoughtfully, and remarked that a few years earlier I would not have been permitted to teach at this school. Did he mean before Nigerian independence? I couldn't understand what he was talking about, decided that he must mean that as a woman I'd have been unwelcome. After all, there were no others on the staff. Roy saw the question on my face and said it was because I was an R.C., a papist; it was my religion that would have barred me from teaching at this school. I was completely baffled. This was the first time I'd encountered the term "R.C." and I understood it only from the context. Nor had I ever heard the word "papist" spoken aloud, and certainly not applied to myself. The very word sounded odd to me, from another age and time, conjuring dangerous outsiders, conspirators plotting to blow things up. Did he recognize me as Irish-American? C. had been brought up as a Protestant of an indeterminate kind, moving between churches as he was growing up, but no longer practiced religion of any sort. Yet he was tolerant of mine and happy enough to accompany me sometimes in my own practice, just as he pleased. It seemed, however, he didn't stand out egregiously, as did I, who, some days after our arrival, had inquired if there was a Catholic church nearby. It was clear my question had made the rounds. Whatever else, I understood that from Roy's point of view I was one of those, like the newly independent Nigerians, who'd been reluctantly permitted through the gate at last.

Then, soon enough, introductions were over, the boys returned to the compound, and classes began. Neither of us had ever entered a classroom as a teacher, had only a few months earlier sat at desks nailed to the floor in classrooms at Columbia where we'd met while studying for master's degrees, where I was first drawn to C.'s mix of spontaneity and reserve, his lean grace refined by years of playing basketball. The first time we sat down together, for coffee, he told me he was going to Africa. Although his desire for travel wasn't at all unusual among the students we knew, it seemed to me he took it as a matter of course that he would soon be living in Africa, a quiet confidence I hadn't encountered before. Europe was one thing, Africa another. His dark eyes looking at me across the table were opaque, I didn't know how to read them. But I already knew they could suddenly dissolve in tenderness. We walked out onto the street, then, and soon he'd disappeared around the corner on his bike, leaning into the curve. The night before, on College Walk, we'd passed each other in the October dusk; our eyes had met and neither of us had looked away.

Mr. Olatunbosun had already told us our youngest students would be about twelve, my age exactly when Miss Hughes had been my music teacher, when Norman de Carteret had been my classmate. But there the teacher-student parallel ended. We discovered that the oldest boys we were to teach, nineteen or twenty years old, were only three or four years younger than we were. They were in upper sixth form, equivalent perhaps to our first or second year of college, and were preparing for what we soon learned to call the higher school certificate exams. With them we read and discussed *Macbeth*, *Great Expectations*, *The Mill on the Floss*. We were the English teachers but didn't seem to know our own language. When the Tulliver aunts engaged in lively conversation in the opening chapters of *The Mill on the Floss*, I had no idea what they were talking about. The first time I'd read the novel myself, it hadn't mattered; I'd simply skipped over the dialogue I couldn't make out. Like my students, like the gypsies Maggie had tried to run away with, I didn't belong to this world. Nor did I always understand the most basic vocabulary. For example, I didn't know that a "row" meant a fight, and pronounced it to rhyme with "toe"; but the boys, seeing my confusion, taught me to pronounce it to rhyme with "cow." I remembered that we'd been told by a teacher from England that there were those who'd objected to the school's hiring Americans as teachers of the English language. The wife of one of the staff had asked us please not to split our infinitives in front of her children.

But then C. and I, Americans who came from different parts of our own country, sometimes pronounced words differently, used different idiom, a fact that charmed me. We might be eating lunch, for example, when suddenly a sheet of water in the doorway, a heavy drum on the roof of the house, led C. to observe that it was "pouring the rain."

III

For the first time, too, the students were reading not only novels by English writers but a novel published only four years earlier by an African. In fact, by a Nigerian: Chinua Achebe. *Things Fall Apart* had for the first time that year been established as a set text for the exam. We'd never read an African novel ourselves and were no more familiar with the culture it described than the one we read about in nineteenth-century English novels. But here we had informants, people to explain things to us, people who were living in the place and moment. Our students, many of whom were Igbo like Okonkwo, the protagonist, came from the eastern region of Nigeria. They told us of course how to pronounce the names of all the characters but could explain other things as well: the meaning, for example, of *ogbanje,* as the child, Ezinma, was thought to be, a changeling who dies again and again, returning each time to her mother. They knew because they'd seen the markings—made in an earlier life—on the bodies of children who'd returned. They could tell us about gestures and ceremonies described in the novel, the exacting rituals around the sharing of that most meaningful symbol of hospitality, the kola nut; could describe their own memories of the betrothals of their older brothers or sisters, the gathering called the *uri* when the dowry is paid. They related stories they'd heard from their elders about the arrival of Europeans in Igboland. They had quite recent memories themselves of local District Commissioners. What our students didn't go into was what I learned only from the book itself: the devastation their people had suffered at the hands of the Europeans. Okonkwo had been robbed of his authority, of his history, of everything that connected him to his ancestors. He had been brutally humiliated and driven to despair. The fabric of his life had been torn asunder by a tribe from afar that imposed its will by means of firearms and churches and jails and that never questioned the superiority of its own traditions, its language and religion. It was this understanding I took from *Things Fall Apart,* and although the class reading occupied only a few weeks' time, Okonkwo's story threw its long shadow over all that I observed around me in the months ahead and threw it backwards, too, over things that had happened before.

Every morning a boy flung a handbell up and down and the day began in the chapel singing hymns composed during the eighteenth century by the Wesley brothers. The students filed in and sat in the front pews. The masters almost all wore white shorts and ironed shirts, and some, white knee socks. The boys' uniform was similar, shorts and shirts, but in khaki: for dress they wore ties and navy blue jackets with the Igbobi insignia sewn to the pocket. Bata sandals for everyone. Sometimes immediately after chapel, under the glossy leaves of the mango tree that made a broad ring of shade just outside, the assistant headmaster, Mr. Esubiyi, caned a boy. The boy bent over and the stick came down on his khaki-clad buttocks. Occasionally he flinched. Usually he did not. Mr. Esubiyi's head, smooth as an egg, gleamed with sweat.

Igbobi College was a distinguished school, we were given to understand. It was on the English public school list along with Eton and Harrow because it had once had a headmaster who'd been headmaster of a public school in England. A public school, a school for those who could pay. These were mysteries we couldn't unravel. What we did understand was that some privilege was being claimed for the school where we taught. Igbobi College had a long and distinguished history, it seemed, and many of our students' fathers had been scholars there not so long before, and still recited stories about Mr. Esubiyi. We were informed that a good number of Igbobi College's graduates were highly placed in the government and in the professions throughout Nigeria. Even now, several of its school-leavers were studying in universities in the UK, in America, and even in Russia. Umenne, for example, the school's champion tennis player whom I'd seen rolling the tennis courts in the afternoon, was bound for Moscow, where he would study engineering.

During the evenings, sometimes, we went into Lagos. We'd bought a used Deux Chevaux, a car that had appealed to C. because it was advertised as "Cartesian even in nuts and bolts." If you were crossing the desert or example, you could remove the front seats at night and sit out under the stars. Leaving Igbobi on our excursions, we swept past the schoolrooms, open on one side, where the boys sat row by row in their study hall. C. drove and I looked out the window. At the sight of the boys bent over their books in the glow of a pale electric bulb I experienced a sharp sense of relief, a joyous realization that the schoolroom had been left behind, that at last I'd been released into the world of adults. And there was a kind of thrill, too, about going out as a couple into the large world, discussing everything when we returned. We might be attending the performance of a new play by Wole Soyinka, *The Lion and the Jewel.* Or have been invited to a party at the American Embassy in Ikoyi where we met people we'd scarcely been aware existed before now: employees of Texaco, Peace Corps doctors and directors, African journalists, visiting ambassadors and diplomats. And colonial officers, too, who'd decided to stay on in Nigeria after independence, working on dictionaries, anthropological studies.

Once, at about the time we were first reading *Things Fall Apart,* we saw that Chinua Achebe was giving a talk in Lagos. We arrived early, sat near the front. There he was, a man only a decade or so older than ourselves, a young man in his early thirties who said that he was afraid for the soul of Nigeria.

It was not the increasing political conflict he most feared in
the new Nigeria. Conflict was utterly predictable given the
fact that Nigeria was an artificial state that had been cobbled
together to suit colonial need: the old principle of divide and
conquer had set one people against another, had fostered
indirect rule. Yes, it was a fabricated nation where groups with
entirely different languages and religions and customs now
struggled to align themselves as compatriots. Everyone knew
that the Muslim Hausa from the savannahs of the north and
the coastal people of the south formerly had little to do with
each other. No, it was not tribal conflict that most worried
Achebe, although the growing corruption of political leaders
might illustrate the point he wished to make. To convey his
worst fear he would tell us a story he'd recently heard from a
friend.

A man driving down the Ikorodu road, it seems, had
passed someone lying beside the road, someone hit by a car.
The driver hadn't stopped, he'd explained later, because he
was afraid that the injured man, if lifted into his car, might
leave bloodstains on his new seat covers. He'd felt no need
to apologize, no need to feel ashamed. It was a culture of
money that was growing in Nigeria, a new emphasis on
personal wealth. Of course there'd always been a tendency to
view power in terms of riches, but now without the play of
traditional values that had connected one person to another
and to the group, as in the precolonial days, there seemed no
limits to self-interest, to the tendency to regard someone else
exclusively in the light of one's own personal imperatives.

The days were passing, we were beginning to know the
rhythms. Before the bell rang for chapel at seven-thirty we
had descended the dappled gray stairs and taken our places

at the heavy table where Ben had already turned our cups upside down on their saucers to keep out the flies. The fan was already turning slowly overhead. Tiny iridescent sunbirds hung in the red hibiscus that flared in the windows. Ben carried in the teapot from the kitchen and put before us plates of toast turned in bacon drippings, fried eggs, beans, cooked tomatoes: an unthinkable breakfast until recently. We were in the classroom from eight until eleven, when there was a half-hour break; then back again until one-thirty, when classes were over for the day and everyone retired for a midday meal. We knew by now the boys ate at long tables in the dining hall—jolof rice, fufu made from pounded yam or cassava, stew with tomato sauce, fried plantain, gari— then rested in their bunks in the dormitories, mosquito nets hanging in clouds above them. Our own lunch we ate beneath a fan turning at a rapid clip: *Gloriosa superba* adrift in the blue glass bowl in the middle of the table. Ben might bring us avocados gathered from the ground beneath the tree we could see through the door, avocados cut in half and filled with the tiny prawns he'd bought in the market; afterwards a wedge of papaya, orange flesh glistening with black seeds, a slice of lime to squeeze on it. Then we climbed the stairs to take a short rest on our bed, stupefied by the heat, reading, making love, dozing. About three-thirty, the voice of a boy called from below: games were beginning. Cricket, soccer, tennis. The boys and men set off for the playing fields and courts.

In the evenings, after Ben had served us dinner, after we'd talked together awhile when we'd finished eating—he standing on one foot, the toes of the other resting on top of it, we reclining in our chairs—after he'd told us something more about the village where he'd grown up in Igboland, stories we eagerly listened to in the hope of further illuminations into the depths of Okonkwo's tragedy, and that C. listened to as well for certain Igbo words he'd heard spoken by the boys and remembered, after Ben had explained more fully how he'd received the scar on his left thigh fighting for the British in Burma during the last war, or related another episode in his career as cook on the Elder Dempster mail boats that moved up and down the coast of West Africa, stopping in Accra, Monrovia, Freetown, Las Palmas, we mounted the stairs to the sitting room where we prepared for the next day's classes and corrected the boys' maroon exercise books stamped with the Igbobi insignia.

That is, if we hadn't been invited out. A lively world of dinner parties was in full swing on the compound—we were asked to "come round" in the evening to one of the bungalows—and soon enough with Ben's help we began inviting people ourselves. We might have a roasted chicken with plantain sliced on the angle, fried in palm oil; or a groundnut stew with its accompanying side dishes of shaved coconut, banana, oranges. I might try out a cold cucumber soup, using the dried milk kept in the food safe that stood in the kitchen, its four legs planted in little tins of water to deter the ants. Dinner parties were entirely new, distinctly grown-up affairs; they'd certainly played no part in our student days. I'd associated adult dinner parties with alcohol, but at Igbobi College spirits were officially allowed nowhere on the compound. We drank filtered water; occasionally Nigerian Star beer made a discreet appearance. This was a "Christian" college, founded by a mission, and I already knew that "Christian" did not include Catholics; the cultures differed in ways that sometimes made for confusion. We'd been asked out for dinner on a Friday night and a little piece of fish had been quietly placed beside my plate. But Vatican II was in full

swing: all that had been swept away. I hadn't registered the
little dish, helped myself to a chop, then looked around and
seen there weren't enough to go round.

And how not to notice the difference between dinner
parties when Nigerian teachers and their wives were included
and those when they were not? The sense, when Europeans sat
alone, of being *en famille*? The conversation, the tone of voice,
was not the same. There would be the inevitable references
to pre-independent Nigeria and how things had stood then;
the deplorable decline in even so short a period. Sometimes to
our own dinners we invited the Nigerian teachers and their
wives, sometimes we were invited to dinner in return. And as
time went on, we were increasingly invited by the families of
our students to gatherings where we were the only Europeans
present. But in those early days there wasn't much mixing,
not between Europeans and Nigerians, nor for that matter
between men and women. At dinner parties of whatever
description, there was preliminary scattered talk about the
washed-out roads now that the rainy season was ending, about
how many weeks of term still remained before the holiday,
about what you could buy where and at what price, and then
the conversation settled down to the real topic of the evening:
Igbobi College. The men talked about students, about school
policies, about considerations that had surrounded the
choice of Mr. Olatunbosun as headmaster. The women were
consigned to an onlooker's silence. I was unsure where to place
myself. I spent my days in the classroom with the boys—not
exactly a master but anyway a teacher—and attended all the
faculty meetings. The boys had begun to fill my thoughts, my
dreams: Sobomowo frowning as he delivered his opinions on
the ghost of Banquo, Kpaduwa and Nwoye interrupting each
other as they argued over whether *Things Fall Apart* could
have been set in a Yoruba village. Or Cole, who distinguished

himself one day by spontaneously rising from his seat and reciting from memory the third act of *Macbeth*, taking all the parts in turn. So when, at these dinner parties, the men talked about our students, I was eager to join in. But at the same time anxious that by doing so I was isolating myself from the other women, maybe even alienating them. I spent my days with men and boys, met the wives of other teachers only occasionally. They were kind to me, but distant. When one evening a woman named Rhoda called me "love" as she passed a dish of boiled potatoes, sudden tears stung my eyes. I hadn't realized how deeply I missed the company of women who till very recently had filled my life.

IV

Then, during those first months at Igbobi College, I became pregnant and a rapid shift took place. After we'd announced our news, I was immediately befriended by the wives of the teachers from England, all of whom had babies or small children of their own. They eagerly lent me books on natural childbirth, instructed me on the value of breathing exercises that would help me through. As to where the baby might be born, they explained the options. There was Dr. Odianju at the Lagos Island Maternity Hospital: that's where the kind Rhoda had recently delivered her little girl. There was as well the clinic in Abeokuta run by a Polish doctor. Which would it be? They described in some detail their experiences of childbirth at one or the other, stories that frightened me. An unexpected breech, three days in labor. Electricity that had gone out in the delivery room just as the baby was about to be delivered, restored only half an hour later. But these were my sisters, the ones who offered the help I was only beginning to suspect I would need. I was grateful for their attention but often mortally embarrassed by their questions in company. I did not want the men to know I'd disappeared suddenly from my class one morning at the onset of a wave of nausea.

Now, during the long afternoons devoted to games, I was sometimes invited for tea at one bungalow or another. This was the hour when the British women gathered with their little walking children and their babies. While the infants were deliriously admired and the toddlers ran about, the mothers took turns telling stories of colic, tantrums, potty training, offering each other reassurance, remedies. Each listened closely while the others spoke, all the time hanging on the moment, it seemed to me, when she would be given the chance to talk about her own child. I had no stories to tell, was struck by the air of rapt, intense preoccupation. I noticed that sometimes a mother would describe the character of her child while the child was standing nearby—he's nothing like his father, she's one of the quiet sort—and I obscurely worried for the child, vowed this I will not do, fix my baby in words. With the teapot, little iced cupcakes often appeared, sandwiches, a jar of marmite, assorted biscuits, a teacake; we were given a choice of squash to drink: orange or lemon. The children, who were being fed for the evening, were taught to address each of us as "auntie" in combination with our first name. The men were, correspondingly, "uncle." We were members of one family, it seemed, one tribe, who were all called European. A German woman who lived on a neighboring compound and was married to a Nigerian came with her baby. She was auntie as well.

But I couldn't see that the talk ever touched on anything other than children. I had no friends who'd had children already so I didn't know anything about women who had.

They didn't talk among themselves at all as I was used to doing with my friends: we told stories about ourselves, mostly. Scrutinized our lives, imagined our futures aloud. Perhaps I didn't know these new companions well enough to make a judgment. Wasn't intimate enough with them to understand. Or perhaps this is what happened to women once they had children. They no longer talked about themselves. But again I made a promise for the future: this will not happen to me.

Sometimes I accompanied Sheila, a woman who seldom appeared at these gatherings, as she wheeled her baby in a pram around the compound in the late afternoons. Her other children—a boy, Patrick, who wore Christopher Robin sandals and strode along with his toes pointing out, a dimpled little girl, Ruth—ran before us on the sandy road. Lizards skittered across our path, stopped short, flexed up and down on squat legs, shot off in another direction. Sheila was a beautiful woman with deep-set eyes, reserved, passionate. She didn't ask what I considered prying questions but I knew she would, if asked, thoughtfully respond to my own uncertainties. Our conversation came in fits and starts. I would ask her the name of a flower or plant. She would exclaim over the beauty of a flock of yellow wagtails, all pecking in the grass, facing the same way. Or she pointed out a white-bellied crombec, along the edge, flitting from spot to spot.

One day, as we were slowly passing one of the tennis courts, she stopped in her tracks. We had been observing a pair of older boys slam the ball back and forth on the red clay, listening to the ping of the ball on the tight gut string. Now, between sets, one of them had gone to the side of the court to retrieve his water flask. Sheila's eyes were on the other, Uranta, standing at rest.

"Look at the line of his arm as he holds his racquet," she exclaimed. "Gorgeous!" And we both gazed, enthralled.

I filed away this new knowledge, relieved. You could be married and unabashedly, openly admire other men. It seemed you need fear no contradiction, suffer no scruple. I was full of curiosity about Sheila's own marriage, wondered what she would say if I asked her about it. Which of course I knew her too little to do. But I was deeply curious about marriage in general, the stories people told. So far, I hadn't heard any. Sheila had been married eight years and her husband, Simon, among the teachers, was our particular friend. We thought his wit of the order of Dudley Moore's in *Beyond the Fringe*. Mad dogs and Englishmen. He was droll, reveled in the absurdity of the situation, put on a serious face as he aped nonsense bandied about at staff meetings. He made fun of the former British high commissioner, of himself standing in front of a classroom, a goon. "Crikey!" he'd exclaim, confronted with some new pomposity. We were certain he noted our own peculiarities, national gestures of body and mind and speech that gave us away, ones we knew were still hidden from ourselves. Simon called Sheila his darling. There was no sarcasm in his voice then.

V

But more often than not—after C. had departed for the cricket field or to help Umenne push the heavy roller over one of the tennis courts that had been damaged by rain—I spent the afternoon hours on the upstairs verandah, reading. Sitting there in the canvas sling-backed chair, I could gaze out over a wide field of grass traversed by an avenue that led through the gates of the school to the Surulere road beyond. I might look up from my book to see a woman walking beneath the shade of the trees that lined the avenue, a baby on her back, a tray on her head heaped with bananas, mangoes. Or a vendor employed by the vice-principal's wife, Mrs. Esubiyi, pushing a cart of Wall Ice Cream that he sold on concession, returning with the proceeds. There might be a student in the high grass, swinging a cutlass, doing the work on the compound all the students were required to take part in. Or, further away, at the edge of the field, a Fulani in a pointed straw hat passing with a herd of skinny white cattle. If I remembered to listen, I could hear drumming, the constant tattoo that often went unnoticed, the beat that ran along beneath the words on the page. The sun was still bright in the sky and then all at once it seemed to have begun a swift descent. The playing fields were growing silent, the air murky. Soon it was dark. A car entered the compound, moving slowly along the avenue, its headlights illuminating a path along the pocked dirt road.

I read till I could no longer make out the words, till the mosquitoes were thick around my ankles. Too much had happened too quickly, I didn't know where I was or what I was doing. The printed page was a place to ponder my life without looking at it directly. For the first time I was numbered among the adults, was no longer a student, had a job that paid my way. I was a teacher, I was married, was going to have a baby, was living in a country distant from my own. My prolonged adolescence was over. School had gone on and on: we'd been waiting for life to begin, my friends and I. What would we do? What was waiting to happen to us? The future was already laid out, we knew that, but still altogether hidden. Now, it seemed, I was on the other side. Alone among my friends I'd married. I was in the midst of it, whatever we'd called life. I reveled in my new freedoms, my new delights.

Yet when I read my friends' letters, I experienced a pang. The fact of marriage had isolated me. Everything that before had seemed so tedious, so lengthy, in no time at all had been transformed into the irretrievable past. The liberties attached to wandering alone were no longer mine. My friends were meeting in foreign places, sharing apartments, becoming close to people I'd never heard of. They wrote of a rendezvous in Paris, a job at the *International Herald Tribune*, a quick trip to Rouen to join a man picked up in a café.

The books I read those long afternoons when the season of rain was coming to an end were borrowed from the bookshelves of bungalows we visited for dinner parties or for the eleven o'clock morning break when coffee was served with Carr's wheat biscuits and slices of cheese. Or the books might have been purchased at Kingsway, the store in Lagos that carried a large selection of paperbacks, Penguin Modern Classics. There was Robert Graves's *Goodbye to All That*, Amos Tutuola's *The Palm Wine Drinkard*, Isak Dinesen's *Out of Africa*. Graham Greene's *The Heart of the Matter*, Camara Laye's *The African Child*, E. M. Forster's *A Passage to India*. Most of the pages I read touched on the sudden translation of my life. Like *Things Fall Apart*, they seemed to tell of a lost place, a passing moment contemplated from afar. I thought I heard the sound of farewell in all of them. There had been something and now there wasn't. The world I'd left so abruptly and from this distance mourned was summoned and swept away again in the comings and goings evoked in *Goodbye to All That*, the friends who were so lively and full of passion now living elsewhere, lost to view. But as I read on, aimlessly, picking up one book and then another, lingering on a sentence, a paragraph, then closing the book to look out over the field in front of me, some shift was taking place.

Until coming to Africa, it seemed I'd spent much of my time deep in the pages of some book. Along with the sense of waiting for life to begin that I'd shared with my friends, I'd harbored a secret terror while I was in school that I could find no words for and that I confided to no one: alone among us I was destined never to have a life at all, any life other than one in books and in reading. I would read my way to the grave and then it would be over. Reading was the only thing I knew how to do. Did I do so for refuge? For reasons too obscure to examine?

But I understood there was a way of living that was not in books. I read about it. It had to do with taking what was offered by the world itself. Of choosing. The novels I found absorbing were often about characters who struggled to do that, sometimes with great difficulty. This life outside of books involved taking chances, risking unhappiness. It meant leaving books behind. It meant risking abandonment and misery.

Now, it seemed, I'd been carried into the life I feared, regardless. It was not that I'd planned to go to Africa, it was simply that the man I'd married—before I met him—had been walking down a gray wet street in London on his own first trip abroad and passed an African who was wearing, over one shoulder, a strip of golden kente cloth. The encounter had lasted no more than an instant but when it was over the resolve had been taken: Africa. This story seduced me. I marveled that a decision might be made with the speed of lightning. And so was inspired to make my own. The person I would marry had translated a passing impulse into plans for a journey of unnumbered days. I would join him in his wanderings.

But C. didn't rush to tell me this story. I was only to learn of it weeks after we'd met when I asked at last why he'd fixed on Africa. Why did he want to go to Africa? It was in part because of his reticence about describing this encounter in the streets of London that I trusted his story. I didn't see anything self-dramatizing about it. He spoke almost reluctantly about an elusive motive that reverberated for me as the very truth.

Sitting on the verandah, listening to the shy beat of happiness in the fluttering drums, I felt the old terror subside. Soon there would be a child. How to share the human lot more profoundly, I wondered, than to bear a child? Some divide had been crossed. And yet, looking down at the pages open on my lap, I had to consider that once more I was trying to read myself into where I was, trying to make out the pattern beneath the astonishing shifts and changes. I knew it had indeed been Africa—from a passing appearance on a rainy day in London to this evening's stretch of rugged grass lit by the first fireflies—that had carried me from the library in which I'd discovered *Lucy Gayheart* into what I now called "my life." But I couldn't understand what it all meant, this surprising twist of fate. Perhaps it had been written somewhere that despite everything that had happened to me earlier I would find myself exactly here, in my twenty-third year, at Igbobi College, in Yaba, just outside Lagos, a spot on earth that until recently I had not known existed. But why this place? Why here?

Slowly, turning the pages of the book as I sat looking out—musing on Camara Laye's African boy growing up in his sun-struck village in upcountry Guinea, achingly recalled in Paris; or thinking about Scobie, in a Monrovia of Graham Greene's imagining, impaled on a fear of doing harm—it began to seem that being in Africa meant being in a place I was already beginning to care for blindly, as indeed for the baby growing within whose face I had not yet glimpsed. And because it seemed this continent I still knew so little about would come to be loved beyond what I could now imagine— or so I felt dimly, the light failing on the page, the cries rising from below of boys returning from the playing fields, the shutters knocking against the side of the house downstairs as Ben opened the dining room for the evening meal—I knew it to be a world that, like all the others I was reading about, would one day be lost. For the first time I was conscious of being greedy for the day, for the world where I was. Each day lived was one day less.

As I was putting my book aside, one evening, aware suddenly of C.'s return, of his voice below speaking with Ben, of Ben's abrupt laughter, I vowed I would at some unknown point in the future record the scent of this dusty twilight, the gleam of trumpet flowers along the stairs, the shuffle of C.'s sandals as he started up the first flight to the landing. The overflow of this raw new happiness would need to be translated into words, words as ordained as what I was calling my life. This was a new thought, the idea of writing things down, of looking within myself for the pattern behind things that were happening to me. And, looking around quickly to fix the moment, I promised myself I would not forget.

VI

One night, after the rains had all but disappeared, when we were sitting upstairs—reading student exercises and writing the little blue aerogrammes we sent home with our news—suddenly, breaking into the silence, steps sounded from below. A hurricane lamp came swinging up in the darkness. Our new friend, Simon, stood at the door. He said he was afraid he had bad news for us. He pushed open the wooden screened frame and stepped inside, carefully closing it behind him. He sat down. He placed the lamp on the floor. He paused. He looked at one of us, then at the other.

"Your president has been shot," he slowly pronounced.

Shot! He told us in stages.

No, John F. Kennedy wasn't injured. No, he wasn't in hospital. He was dead, Simon said. People were weeping in the streets. We didn't understand what Simon was saying. He was sorry but no, unfortunately there was no mistaking it. He had been listening to the BBC and the news had come in.

But where was all this happening? The place where JFK had been hit by a bullet while he sat in a limousine with Jackie driving through the streets of Dallas, waving his hand at the crowds, had no reality. Neither of us had ever been to Dallas. Nor were there any images to make this appalling story real. What was real was the lantern on the floor next to Simon's feet in his buckled sandals, the maroon exercise books with the Igbobi insignia stamped on the covers littering the room.

It was only hours later, waking to the harsh throb of the night, looking out into the still-dark leaves of the frangipani tree in the window, that I swooned in wonderment, asking myself how I could bring a human being into the world, the child already growing in my womb. The world was too terrible a place. What was the use?

The next day the boys in the classrooms fell silent when we appeared, they watched us pass. Our colleagues told us they shared our grief. With some embarrassment we received condolences. Our new importance, our dignity as mourners, was not unwelcome, but there were aspects that worried us. Despite our deep sadness and confusion, we had always considered ourselves half-hearted patriots. We had wished to distance ourselves from our country, as it suited us, to enjoy the luxury of voluntary displacement. Yet we could find no reflection of our own ambivalence in the faces of others. On the contrary, we were walking testimony that such a place existed. "America," everyone called it, a mythic name we didn't recognize; the name of a book, spelled with a "K." A song from *West Side Story*. Yes, we were Americans, but the United States is what we called the country we came from.

A couple of days later, as I was putting my books together following a lower-sixth-form class—sixteen-, seventeen-year olds, I'd learned—Ajayi and Ogundele approached my desk. Both earnest students, both from the town of Abeokuta, they were known to be good friends, were often seen walking about the compound together, arms around each other's shoulders. Ajayi had a single tiny tribal mark on the highest point of each cheekbone; his eyes were far apart and his expression windswept, open. In class he was mostly silent. Ogundele, small and excitable, wore horn-rimmed glasses at all times and put up his hand for only a moment before irrepressibly calling out what was on his mind. We had that day spent the hour on vocabulary drills in preparation for reading *Great Expectations*, but I knew these friends would be making their own lists of new words they liked to spill at odd moments, savoring the sounds. Now I thought they'd approached as they sometimes did to confirm a meaning, a pronunciation.

Instead Ajayi slowly took a newspaper from beneath the

books he was carrying. He unfolded it and laid it out on the desk, a journal printed the day before in Lagos. Its headlines appeared in bold ink: "Some U.S. Whites Still Hate Blacks." Ogundele looked at me, deeply serious, eyes enlarged by the lenses of his glasses, and asked if I thought this was the reason for the assassination of my president. Shaking my head in wonder, looking from one to the other, I said I didn't understand. Ajayi delicately kept his eyes fixed on the words, as if to spare me. But I could only look blankly at the boys, deeply confused, and as the bell rang to mark the beginning of the next class they'd walked silently away.

At lunch, beneath a briskly turning fan, I at once told C. about the headlines. What could this mean? But he shook his head, as mystified as I. We didn't have a radio so relied on others to tell us what was happening. Had we missed some piece of news that would have made something clear? We couldn't understand how race had anything to do with the assassination. After all, it wasn't a black man who'd been assassinated. It hadn't been Martin Luther King.

Yet it seemed our students knew about the world we'd left behind in ways we hadn't been aware. Knew about things we'd scarcely absorbed ourselves because we were entirely satisfied not to. We may have been squeamish about expressions of patriotism, yet even so, ironically, we had assumed that as Americans we would be recognized as carrying with us a refreshing freedom from the old dispensations, old tyrannies, would be recognized by an openhearted generosity toward others. Our country we thought was exceptional in its acceptance of difference.

Now it broke on us slowly, and then more quickly, in a headlong sweep, that we had been astonishingly innocent. Peering out from behind the bright armor of our complacency, we'd given little thought to what others already knew about us. It was the old human failing. We'd wished to be seen as vanity dictated.

"Some Americans Still Hate Blacks." I began to put things together only after inquiring directly, one morning, of a Nigerian colleague who taught history at Igbobi. John Sagay wore a dashiki and long pants, had studied in London, spoke slowly and softly but with unmistakable intent. We'd been told that—although often asked—he declined invitations to dinners on the compound given by Europeans. Meeting him in the staff room where we picked up our mail, I'd hesitantly approached and asked about the headlines that Ajayi and Ogundele had shown me. He regarded me thoughtfully for a moment and then, shifting the student notebooks he was carrying from one arm to the other, pronounced the word "Birmingham." With a sudden brilliant smile he mentioned tribal conflict in the country I came from. He asked if there hadn't been a recent push there to pass civil rights legislation. When I continued to look blank, he reminded me—as if to spell things out—that President Kennedy had belatedly supported that legislation. It was then that comprehension broke over me like a wave, and I thanked him. He'd nodded at me, lifting his eyebrows as if to acknowledge what had passed between us.

It was only later that I saw what might have been obvious from the beginning: news is inevitably written from the point of view of the one reporting. If we hadn't been aware of this fact while we were in our own country, it was because whatever the editorial differences between the papers we were used to reading, they had shared the same historical perspective. A white president, for instance, would not have been shot because he was promoting, if somewhat reluctantly, a civil rights agenda. There would be other reasons considered more important. Conspiracy theories might spin but civil rights would not be at the heart of them. Unless of course you saw things through a different lens, the lens of race, unless that was your concern. Unless you were African or the descendant of Africans.

From the first, we'd had misgivings. If we hadn't wanted to be seen as "helping," it was because we knew that what people called good intentions often disguised more sinister ones. The white race—the original Europeans, that is: not Americans like ourselves—had behaved appallingly in Africa. We'd read not only *Things Fall Apart* but as students had studied Conrad's *Heart of Darkness*, been taught that the title referred to the human will to power. In this instance, the vicious machinery of King Leopold's "sacred mission of civilization" in the Congo, where European lust for ivory had led to the unspeakable. To severed heads, I remembered, stuck up on poles. To Kurtz's unleashed pride, to ruthless control of his little kingdom where anything was possible. And yet even a few months in Nigeria had raised questions about the darkness we'd been assured by our teachers was symbolic. Why were "the blacks" presented in Marlowe's tale as savages, rolling their eyes, howling? Whatever the reason, the book would never do for our Igbobi classrooms. That was clear.

Nor, for that matter, would Isak Dinesen's, with its portraits of noble Africans indispensable to a dream of the European settler's charmed life in Kenya, its code of noblesse oblige, its loyal servants figuring as retainers, as standard bearers, as pages. No, I couldn't imagine Sobomowo or Oridota making much of Kumante, the Kikuyu boy-cook, preparing Cumberland sauce for the Prince of Wales, or of Denys Finch-Hatton setting off on safari. Lear raving on the heath, yes. The black Moor's consuming jealousy, yes. But *Out of Africa*, with its high, knowing pronouncements about "the Native," would not have charmed our students.

Times had changed and soon—in fact in only a few months' time—Kenya would be independent. There'd been reports, recently, of detention camps where thousands of Kikuyu—suspected of having taken part in the Mau Mau rebellion—had been imprisoned, had died of torture, abuse, starvation. It was said more than one thousand alone had been summarily hanged. All of that, I thought, had been the other side of the tapestry, the knotted, incoherent side, where the shadow of a raised whip could be made out against the beautiful hills of Ngongo.

Out of Africa was not purged of vanity, it seemed; that was the difficulty. There was some idea of self that demanded compliance, submission. And here I remembered, uneasily, that very recently I'd told myself some little story about "falling in love" with Africa. But what had I meant? Some dream was being spun in the air, one that would have consequences. What were its ingredients, necessities? I could not forget that my fancies had taken shape to the sound of the shutters below clapping against the side of the house as Ben opened the dining room. A pleasant reminder that my reading could continue undisturbed, that without any trouble at all I'd soon descend to a dinner of steak and kidney pie.

In the interests of the complicated pleasures of the moment, however, I'd been happy to dismiss these misgivings. It was altogether simpler to fetch up another book from the pile at my feet, *A Passage to India*, to look up from its pages and listen for the pock pock of the cricket ball hitting a bat in a nearby field, to tell myself a somewhat different story: "I'm witnessing the last of the British Empire," I'd think. "This is the long shadow it throws."

And so I put off reflecting on my own circumstances and turned for distraction and relief to the shadowy figure of the colonial I'd caught sight of in that novel: the suitor who stoops to conquer, whose pride is soothed by annexation, whose appetite for gold and ceremony is appeased by a handsome dowry.

I remembered that on August 28, the day we were getting on a plane in London that would land at the Lagos International Airport, crowds were gathering for the March on Washington; Martin Luther King was perhaps even then preparing the opening of his "I Have a Dream" speech. It had not occurred to us, far away as we were traveling, halfway across the world, that the eyes of the people we would soon meet were fixed on the events we were leaving behind. Earlier that spring, we'd seen the photographs taken in Birmingham. But it had all happened elsewhere: police dogs lunging at demonstrators, whips, hoses, billy clubs, bloodied faces. These were not our compatriots, this was not the country we claimed as ours. It had never occurred to us, simply, that we might be mistaken for the enraged whites we saw in the papers. Could it be that Ogundele—regarding me dreamily from his desk, watching me write on the blackboard—might fleetingly see a raised stick in my hand instead of a piece of chalk?

What we hadn't understood the night of our arrival, embarrassed and appalled by Michael Bowen's behavior towards Ben, was that who we thought we were counted for nothing. Ben would now be our servant. He would address C. as "Master," as he had so many others. Mortified as we were at first, the intense heat quickly served to change our minds. Far from seeing anything amiss in this arrangement, we would come not only to rely on his services, but to harbor a feeling of complacency about them. Although we tried to be generous with gifts, we'd been warned at the outset not to upset the wage scale that prevailed on the compound and in the end paid him no more than what had been set: a bare pittance. How quickly we had accommodated!

Is it only when we catch sight of our own indifference to suffering reflected in the eyes of another that we at last recognize it? When we realize we have been seen? Because now what had seemed obscure, unrelated, came rushing up to the surface like an involuntary blush of shame. I remembered Badagry.

One Sunday a couple of weeks after our arrival in Lagos, in fact the very day before classes were to begin, a young American couple we'd only just met took us with them on a day trip. They'd already taught for a year at a school in Surulere, not far from Igbobi College, and had come up the stairs and knocked on the door a day or two after our arrival. Dave was older than we were, maybe thirty, a little stooped, and at first didn't say much. We told them straight off that the electricity had blinked out for a couple of hours the night before, and Susan offered to take us to a corner of the market where we could buy candles; it would certainly go out again. She had beautiful straight white teeth and a slightly uncertain way of speaking, as if fearful of being contradicted. When we confessed we'd never taught before, had no preparation at all, they'd tried to coach us a little, had given us some suggestions for how we might conduct a first class. They told us about their own students, described exercises that had come out of their teaching. Dave had mapped out a complex graph of

English language syntax, he would show it to us, with all the tenses accounted for. It was then I realized I'd never formally learned the tenses or what they were called.

In fact, it was to take our minds off the anxieties of the opening day that they'd proposed traveling in their car with them to Badagry, an hour's drive along the coast west of Lagos, not far from the border of Dahomey. They knew because they'd visited Badagry once before. We began our trip around noon, left the outskirts of Lagos behind, and were soon looking out at the ocean. From the backseat windows of the car we could see dense banana groves, dark green clusters of notched and ragged leaves, green fruit not dangling but growing straight up, in clumps, could see palm trees bending all in one direction toward the heaving waters of the Bight of Benin. We passed through villages that straddled the road, glimpsed what we knew only to call huts, children who stood staring, waving too, sometimes, as the car passed.

Dave recounted, as we drove along in the stifling car, that all this had once been called the slave coast, that Badagry was one of the first trading ports, was renowned for the number of people who had last seen Africa from this particular stretch of beach. Some of them—Hausas, for instance, he told us— were from inland, from the northern savannahs, and had never glimpsed the ocean: they'd been terrified, had to be forced onto boats. We listened, the sweat running down our faces. Even ten days after our arrival, we woke each morning with the expectation of cooler air, as if this extraordinary heat would surely have passed. Everything seemed to be happening in a kind of haze, as if the edges of the world had become uncertain, not quite in focus.

Now, as we turned onto the road that took us into town, Dave told us that the trade in Badagry had started in the early part of the sixteenth century, a latecomer in ports in the Bight of Benin that went all the way back to the 1480s. At first Badagry had been dominated by Portugal, then by the Netherlands and France.

"Didn't Britain come in there somewhere?" Susan said.

"That is correct," Dave replied. "By the eighteenth century Britain controlled most of the transatlantic trade."

As soon as we arrived in town we found a concession where we bought some bottles of orange Fanta and ate the sandwiches we'd brought with us. We each drank a second bottle of Fanta, holding the frosty bottles against our foreheads. From where we sat, stunned by the heat into silence, we could see the swampy harbor of water, could see the mangrove trees rising out of the depths where salt and fresh water flowed together. Then we made our way to the little museum where we would find what a sign in front called "slave relics." Inside, the keeper of the museum showed us long iron chains hanging from a suspended bar. Some had neck collars attached. He showed us smaller chains used for children. Leg irons. Devices, again made of iron, to seal the lips, to render impossible the pronunciation of a single word. Mouth bits. We read what was written on cards that had been placed beside the exhibits. The mind reeled. The large slave ships waited at a spur of land across the harbor called Departure for the Land of No Return. Slaves were made to climb into smaller vessels and taken there. Then, shackled, they entered the holds of ships that would carry them across the Atlantic to ports in the Americas: Jamestown, Virginia, for instance. Many would die at sea. In the New World those who survived would be sold to owners of cotton or sugar plantations.

The room was small and close. While the keeper stood silently by, we slowly made our way around. Never had any of us been confronted with evidence like this, not in our own country. But why not? Why not in the country of our birth where so many had ended up? The last wall we examined—on which maps and drawings as well as cards were on display—was dedicated to the history of Nigeria. Over the period of the entire transatlantic trade, we learned, more than two million slaves had been shipped from what is present-day Nigeria to the Americas. Most of these slaves were Igbo and Yoruba, but the number had included many Hausas, many Ibibios. All along the coast at slave ports from Lagos to Calabar flags could be seen flying: those of the European maritime countries and the flag of the North American colonies, too.

We left a few coins in the box at the entrance and, nodding to the keeper, stepped out into the hot stiff wind. We crossed the road and stood beneath a tall coconut palm, heavily notched, leaning in the direction of the water. It afforded little shade after all, but I could make out, just beneath the rustling fronds, brown fruit lodged in the dense shadows. Beneath our feet the sand was dark and coarse, granular.

"Too much to take in!" C. said. "Did you see how they were arranged in the holds? Shackled and laid side by side? Like spoons."

No one had any response. What was there to say? I wanted only to be alone, to try to make space inside myself for this spot on earth where these unspeakable events had taken place. What was so unsettling on the beach where we stood was the austere silence, broken only by the wind rattling the dry fronds of the palm trees, the slap slap of tepid water on rough sand. If I were to try to make real what had happened I'd have to imagine voices, thousands and thousands of them, rising and falling over the centuries: some bellowing orders in languages I didn't understand, others moaning, weeping, still others choking on iron bits. Have to imagine whips making bloody stripes across bare backs. A child, perhaps a skinny boy of twelve, stumbling in chains across the sand where we were standing now.

Yet when I made an effort to do so, I felt an irritable need to stop at once, to think of something else. As I had another time when I had come face-to-face with suffering, I couldn't think when. Where on earth was I now? And at what point in my life? I tried to think again of the boy in chains passing over this patch of sand where we stood but could focus only on the black flies biting my ankles, on the sweat running down my face. Later on, I thought, I'd be able to imagine Badagry, perhaps at night when it was cooler.

Susan asked if I'd brought a hat with me, I should be careful in this sun. C., darker-skinned than I, urged me to remain in the shade. I answered that it didn't matter. Why, I asked, didn't we go down to that pier where the slaves had climbed aboard. There were no swimmers in the lagoon, but we could see a few boats at some distance, were able to make out a spur of land stretching beyond. We decided that must be the Point of No Return.

That night my face was hot to the touch, enflamed, puffy. I could scarcely recognize it in the mirror. When I closed my eyes it was not to sleep but to a waking vision of Norman de Carteret standing alone, staring into his locker. I had denied Norman and that betrayal had closed the door on my childhood. After a while I fell asleep and next morning, by the time the rooster crowed beneath our window, my face was so swollen I couldn't smile, could speak only with an effort. At eight o'clock we assembled in front of the chapel for the first time. Inside, Mr. Olatubosun said a prayer and welcomed the students to a new term. He was confident each one would give his studies his whole attention. We sang a Wesley hymn, then the Doxology. I observed I was the only woman in the chapel. Afterward I entered a classroom and was handed a list of the students' names, was instructed to call out each one. The boys sat at little desks, the kind with a lid that opens on a hinge. This was the lower sixth form, the boys were sixteen, maybe seventeen. The legs of some spilled helplessly into the aisles. I began at the top of the page: Yoruba names, I'd been told, Igbo, Hausa.

Abagbe: I made a broken attempt to pronounce the name and the boy named Abagbe responded, calling it out correctly. I tried to repeat what I'd heard. Abeyomi. Abiola. Abubakar. Achebe. Agunwole. Ajayi. Each boy said his name aloud and I did my best to reproduce it, my face aflame, silently appalled that these must have been among the names belonging to those who'd worn the irons I'd seen on display the day before: names that had been taken away from them as soon as they set foot in the "New World." Babafemi. Babatuola, Balewa, Binitie. Cole, that one was easy. So was Davies.

The boys were extremely courteous, waiting patiently till I laboriously reached the end of the list. They were also, I thought, deeply amused. White skin wandering in Africa. Even as I called out their names, I caught sight of little papers shuttling between the desks, written with the names, I thought, they were trying out on me.

A few days after the assassination, again with Susan and Dave, we drove up to Abeokuta, in Ogun state, the town we'd been told Wole Soyinka had come from. Amos Tutuola as well. And of course our students Ajayi and Ogundele. Although we hadn't seen much of them since our trip to Badagry a couple of months earlier, we were glad now to be with other Americans. The line, the shining twisted cable—running between the slave port we'd visited together and the headline in the Nigerian paper following JFK's assassination that some Americans still hated blacks—had become electrically charged. A live connection, hidden till now, glistened and shook. We drove inland, this time, into Yorubaland, on a road through the rain forest. Vast trees, mahogany, walnut, sapele, rose high above what looked like a dense mesh of intensely green forest hung with liana that trailed from branch to branch. It was hard to see the tops of the highest trees because of the dense mid-growth, but in the occasional long shaft of sunlight we glimpsed enormous nervous roots roiling up from the ground. We could see, too, among the roots, plots of land that had been cleared for yam and cassava; the harvest, we knew, had already been gathered. Every once in a while Dave pointed out to us the rusting skeleton of a car by the side of the road, all but hidden beneath a luxuriant growth of bush and vine. A glistening black mamba sped in front of the car, disappeared into the forest.

As soon as we arrived in Abeokuta, we found a place to eat that had a TV. We wanted to watch the news. Everyone's eyes were fixed on it. We stood in the crowd around the bar. Over and over the same image was replayed. A man wearing a hat, seen only from the back, is holding out a pistol, is in the very act of shooting Lee Oswald, the man who'd assassinated JFK. The new assassin's name is Jack Ruby. Lee Oswald is wearing a sweater: in fact he looks like a schoolboy, his shirt collar worn outside his sweater. His face is twisted in anguish, he is clutching his gut. The detective holding Lee Oswald by the arm looks dumbfounded. He is also wearing a hat, a large Texas kind of hat, but Oswald's head is bare. The fact he is not wearing a hat seems to mark him as the one meant to die.

But how could this be, people standing around us asked? We were Americans, could we tell them? Wasn't Oswald already in prison? The people we were watching on TV looked to them like cowboys. Those were cowboy hats they were wearing. Did all this happen in a part of our country where the law was still in the hands of sheriffs? Is that why the president had been shot in the first place? But we were as stunned as they were. We knew nothing, had not even heard yet that Oswald had been shot. Susan lifted her shoulders in disbelief. We were seeing the events on TV only just after they happened. We might have been watching a movie.

VII

The rains were now well behind us. In the mornings the sun, seen through the fine dust that blew down from the Sahara, rose as a round red disk, like the moon. This was the season of harmattan. The evenings were cooler than before although noons were still hot, fiery. The first term was ending. The night before the students were to leave the compound for their month's holiday, a Christmas service was held in the chapel. The ceremony began in total darkness, with a younger boy singing the opening verse of "Once in David's Royal City." When the others joined him, lanterns were placed in the open embrasures in the walls, instantly creating points of light that scattered leaping shadows both inside and out. Mr. Olatunbosun stood before us, greeting us all on the completion of the term, reminding the students that it had been satisfactorily completed for those who'd worked hard and not so satisfactorily for those who had not. He expected that each would return in a few weeks with renewed energy for study. The head boy spoke, wishing a good holiday not only to Mr. Olatunbosun but also to Mr. Esubiyi, the vice-principal, to all the masters, and last but not least to his fellow students. Then followed more English Christmas songs.

For the evening's conclusion, Mr. Amaichi, the music

teacher, had written an Igbo carol, sung now to the accompaniment of Yoruba drums hung with little silver bells that jingled and shook. The drummers, students from the upper forms, bent over their instruments, gathered the strings to tighten the skins or loosen them. These were the talking drums, and the hook of a finger could elicit another tone, some other meaning entirely, as could the flats of the drummers' palms, the fluttering tips of their fingers. Mr. Amaichi stood in front, directing the singers, his arms chopping the air, opening wide the empty spaces. The voices rose high and shrill, following the beat set for them by the drums, insistent, complicated, but sometimes, by way of counterpoint, departing from it entirely. When everything was at its most intense—the drumming, the bells, the sure sliding voices—the music abruptly stopped. In the long silence that followed we could hear the night creatures singing outside, could observe the light thrown by the lanterns across the yellow grass.

During the next days I went out walking with Sheila in the deserted compound. The boys had returned home, and many of the Nigerian and English teachers had taken advantage of the holiday to travel elsewhere. Sheila pointed out to me birds that had returned with the harmattan. Far overhead, we could see black kites circling, distinguished from vultures by their forked tails. They glided great distances, it seemed, heads tilting one way then the other. Patrick, who would soon be six years old, ran far ahead of us, stirring up dust on the road. The sun fell quickly. As dusk came on, Sheila said she was on the lookout for the long-tailed nightjar with its red eye.

Then Christmas Eve. All morning, it had seemed a day like any other, except that C. had been quiet, absorbed by thoughts I couldn't read. When I'd asked if something was wrong, he'd answered briefly that nothing was. I was disconcerted, anxious. At noon, saying scarcely a word, we ate a lunch of cold potatoes with oil and lemon juice drizzled over them, sliced ripe avocadoes and tomatoes, smoked herring from a tin. I didn't know how to coax C. into conversation and with an effort tried to turn my thoughts elsewhere. Ben had stepped down from the raised ledge between the dining room and the causeway holding a plate of thickly sliced toast—to go with the herring, he said—and the sight of his bare feet, the spread of his toes, reminded me of the first time we'd met, not even four months ago, his feet then planted in the same spot as now, head averted to threats leveled at him by a man who knew nothing about him whatsoever. How little we ourselves knew of his life, I thought, and wondered how he'd been addressed by his commanding officer in Burma, by the medics who'd tended the wound in his thigh. Or on the Elder Dempster line going up and down the west coast of Africa by what surely must have been a long line of bosses, by hosts of passengers consuming the meals he cooked, as did we. For the first time I saw myself as part of that great company, as one in a long line, and marveled how much more he knew about all of us than we did of him. He had only to feel our manner toward him to know us more intimately than we knew ourselves.

A year ago this day, I remembered, not only had I been completely unaware that Ben existed in the world, I scarcely knew more of Nigeria than its name, that it was somewhere in West Africa. I had been at my parents' house, distracted, ill at ease, consumed with missing C. The time had clearly come to leave everything behind. It's not that C. and I talked much about Africa: the question was whether or not we'd be together wherever we were. Before Christmas dinner was underway I'd dashed out and taken the train back into the city to meet him. But now, plucked up and set down in a country on the other side of the world, with a husband who at this minute was distracted, I ached for the house I'd grown up in. I ached for the people in it, the shining Christmas tree, the hushed expectancy of the frosty fading afternoon. Nigeria was five time zones ahead of New York and those at home were just now waking to a frigid morning. I half expected that tomorrow would be icy cold, could imagine Christmas no other way.

And then, in the midst of my musings, the fan spinning unheeded overhead, C. got up from the table and, to my bewilderment, disappeared into the hot afternoon.

I first thought that maybe he'd gone through the causeway into the kitchen to speak with Ben, who wouldn't be working tonight or tomorrow. In truth I knew we'd already exchanged good wishes with Ben on the holiday, had already put money into an envelope and given it to him. Or perhaps he'd gone in search of Ben for some information concerning the Igbo greetings: Ben was teaching them to him and they frequently consulted about pronunciation, usage. These were the stories I told myself. I had to make one up to cover C.'s absence, to give myself some reason for it. Idling under the fan, I couldn't think what to do. The red hibiscus in the window lifted their trumpets in the silence of the burning afternoon. An orange-headed lizard hurled himself into the room and stopped short under the chair where C. had been sitting a moment before. At last, stirring myself, I got up to look. The kitchen door was locked, Ben already gone. There was no one. The sun fell through the dusty leaves of the tree beyond, making splotches of light on the sand. In the shade a fallen grapefruit had broken open and lay scattered there, fruit consumed, rind scooped and white as bone.

Upstairs in our sitting room, sprawled on the little sofa, I freely gave myself over to feelings of bleak abandonment. Where was I and what was I doing here? A few cards received from home were propped up here and there on the bookcase, but they seemed at sharp odds with the heat, the melancholy. The crow of a rooster—sudden, piercing—cracked open the solitude of the hour. Clinging with its little padded toes to a corner of the ceiling, its black eyes bulging, a gecko snapped at a fly, slowly consumed it.

And then, suddenly, I was in a rage. It was C. who was to blame for my loneliness! It was Christmas Eve and he'd gone off somewhere. What's more, he hadn't even told me where he was going. He'd walked off without a word! Didn't he understand that I wouldn't want to be left alone? And on this day in particular? I'd counted on his being with me, had never even thought to say anything because I'd taken it for granted we'd spend the afternoon together. Did we know each other at all? Did he know me? The more I thought about it, the more unbearable it all seemed. Tears of outrage stung my eyes. I remembered all over again, looping round as if realizing for the first time, that he hadn't even told me where he was going! Hadn't uttered a single word! Where was he? I had no idea. By this time I'd collapsed into weeping and quickly turned on myself. Good God, what a fool I'd been. What was I doing here? How had I come to find myself in this spot? I had no one to blame but myself. And in a daze of heat and misery and tears, I laid my throbbing head on a scratchy cushion and fell asleep.

But I was about to glimpse that things are sometimes not what they seem. Breaking into my dreams only very gradually, confusedly, came the sound of voices from what seemed a great distance. At first I couldn't remember where I was or what time of day it was. A blaze of light in a window frame, the stem and fronds of a palm outlined in the white heat beyond. A burning pillow. How long had I slept? Good Lord, what had happened! My head was throbbing. Then I located the voices as rising from somewhere else; looking around, I understood them to be coming from the bottom of the stairs. Some little chorus was attempting to sing "We Three Kings of Orient Are." There were false starts, laughter. Then the song gathered, very slowly mounted the stairs, turned at the landing and gravely continued up the last steps: "Bearing gifts we travel afar."

Outside the screened door stood little Patrick, Simon, and C. They opened the door and solemnly followed one another inside, each carrying a little pile of presents. There was exclaiming all round.

"These are for you," C. said, his dark eyes on me, abashed.

But who had wrapped them so carefully in green and brown paper? Who had tied the green ribbons? It was Sheila, Simon said, who'd done that.

They were too beautiful to open right away. I'd keep them until tomorrow morning. So as to have something to look forward to. I gave my own present to C. that night, after we'd returned from St. Dominic's church in Yaba along the Herbert Macaulay Road, after we'd listened to the chorus of high voices singing "Go Tell It on the Mountain," had mounted the stairs to our rooms. I was exhausted from my earlier weeping, heady with relief, and recognized in a flash that what I'd seen as withdrawal in C. had been preoccupation with his surprise for me. We went to bed together that night as if for the first time. But by then I'd already given C. the mask he'd admired a few weeks earlier in the market. It had made him think of the *egwugwu* masks worn by dancing elders, masks described in *Things Fall Apart*, the faces of the ancestral gods that presided over conflict, meting out justice. We'd remembered together that they'd embodied the spirit of the clan and that when they'd been struck to nothing by the court of the district commissioner, by the cut of its whip on an elder's back, the clan's ancient authority and culture had been destroyed. I'd returned and bought the mask from a trader who'd carefully wrapped it in a piece of white cloth and then again in newspaper. I'd tied the whole thing in ribbon so as not to disturb the pungent smell of wood.

I waited until the next morning to open my own presents. There was a black metal paint box that opened and shut with a clasp; inside were little rounds of watercolor as well as three brushes. Accompanying the paint box was a large pad of drawing paper. There was also a bolt of blue cloth bought from a Lebanese merchant to be made by a tailor into a dress: the fuller kind I would need in the coming months. And a string of sandalwood beads that smelled of smoke and gardenia. There was also a seashell C. had picked up in Badagry that we'd handed back and forth between us as we returned in the car to Lagos. And a little straw basket bought in the market where I could keep my earrings and bracelets. Then a box of dark chocolates, each one in the shape of a small bottle containing a drop of liqueur, wrapped in bright foil, gold on the outside, silver within. The last gift I unwrapped was a book. It was a paperback, *The Portrait of a Lady* by Henry James. On the cover was a drawing of a woman sitting in a low chair, hands folded, staring straight out in front of her. Two men, sitting on either side in adjoining seats, were turned toward her. The little logo of the penguin upright in his orange square in the lower right corner was stamped next to the price: 7/9. I quickly turned the book over and read what was printed on the back:

> *The conception of a certain young lady affronting her destiny was how the author described this study of innocence betrayed. The gay, independent, and beautiful Isabel Archer, when she comes to Europe, is courted by several eligible men: she is duped, however, by the spurious charms of Gilbert Osmond, who is encouraged by his mistress to marry Isabel in order to provide for their illegitimate daughter. This poignant story of an American Princess in the toils of European guile is generally regarded as the finest book of James' middle period.*

The Portrait of a Lady

So when I opened the book that Christmas afternoon—settling down in the canvas chair to read, thinking how wonderful such a thing were possible, this gift of time to read a book during the holiday—I already knew what would happen to Isabel. I read quickly, aware almost immediately that as soon as I'd finished the last page I'd have to begin all over again. I'd never read a novel by Henry James and didn't know how to understand this one. Here was a voice quite different from any I'd heard, both grave and lively, given to metaphor. Each sentence seemed charged with a mysterious beauty, an uncanny precision. The story opens on a glorious summer's afternoon, three men having tea on the lush green lawn of a great house in England where the shadows are now beginning to lengthen. But the owners of this house, the people living in it, are not English; they're Americans. Gardencourt—as the house is called—is the property of Mr. Daniel Touchett of Rutland, Vermont, a banker who has lived in England for many years and is now an old man sitting in a cane chair. His son Ralph—witty, ill, intensely sympathetic—is strolling back and forth with his friend Lord Warburton, a neighbor who is visiting for the afternoon. The house is old, beautiful, its bricks glowing in the waning hours of the summer's day; a silver river flows just beyond. A ripeness complete. And into this scene steps from the doorway of the house a young American woman dressed in black, twenty-three, cousin to Ralph, brought by her aunt to Europe. This young woman's name is Isabel Archer. An estrangement has meant that she has never before met this side of her family.

As I quickly turned the pages, moving from one chapter to the next, I was confused as to how I was meant to understand the heroine of the story. Certainly she is charmed by the scene before her, is sensitive to every passing current. Prepared to be pleased, she says what comes to mind. But she seemed to have a quality unusual in the young heroines who appeared in the novels I was used to reading: Isabel had an oddly sharp sense of her own importance, a striking confidence in her theories about life. At once she becomes friends with Ralph, who, when she inquires if there's a ghost at Gardencourt, late on the first night of her stay, replies that it has never been seen by a young, innocent, and happy person like herself. You had to have suffered greatly to see it, he tells her, to have gained some miserable knowledge. He himself has seen it long ago. She replies that she's very fond of knowledge but believes that people suffer too easily, that it wasn't absolutely necessary to do so. That she'd come to Europe to be as happy as possible. And so concluding, takes the candle he hands her and trails up the stairs to bed.

All this seemed a little strange. Why, I wondered, did Isabel, who had seemed so quick, so responsive, make nothing at all of Ralph's confession? Wasn't she even a little curious about his story? Was it some preoccupation with herself and her own ideas that made her obtuse? Some fear of life? Her character seemed full of contradictions. I could see that even as she wants to hurl herself into the scene before her, she is troubled in spirit. She is spontaneous and watchful at the same time. She thinks well of herself, but she is afraid. She is bored, even impatient, with men's habit of falling in love with her. Or seems to be. There is already Caspar Goodwood of Boston, who has ardently pressed her to marry him on the eve of her departure. She will tell him as he pursues her across the ocean that she is very fond of her liberty. Now there is Lord Warburton, the landed proprietor and peer, who has instantly fallen in love with her and has also proposed marriage; to him she says she could never be happy trying to escape the common lot. All this was complicated, interesting: the calm certainty with which she refuses, her sturdy belief in herself.

I was used to giving my sympathy to the heroine of a novel but in this case I couldn't quite. There was something off-putting, it seemed to me, in Isabel's assumption that she was of an altogether superior sort. There was something forbidding in the streak of vanity that ran like a dark vein through all her bright candor. She seemed to find it unsurprising that she was generally admired because, in fact, she considered herself exceptional. She had clearly brought this assurance with her from the other side of the Atlantic. She did not seem innocent to me; she seemed willful, impervious. Her theories, her ideas about happiness, served to protect her from knowledge— of Ralph's illness, for instance—that would have violated something untouched in herself. Or perhaps this was indeed what was called innocence?

I had to put the book aside because soon we'd be making our way, along with the others who had remained on the Igbobi compound, to a Christmas dinner at a bungalow belonging to one of the English teachers. When I'd asked what we could bring, I'd been told to purchase a tin of plum pudding at

Kingsway. I'd made a hard sauce to go with it, but had left out the usual swig of brandy. The couple giving the dinner, Charles and Emily, had lived a long time in Nigeria: in fact, they'd met and married in Lagos, Emily having formerly taught at Queen's College, a girls' school. Now they had a little boy ten months old and had offered to take us with them when they went to Abeokuta to visit the Polish pediatrician at the clinic where their baby had been delivered. Charles was a rumpled, easygoing man, a genial host but, I guessed, hard to know well. Emily was thin and intense, very clever, and told stories with an energy that sometimes seemed driven by nervous fear.

I had Emily to thank for a glimpse into a marriage other than my own. One evening, only a few nights before, at a dinner party on the compound where they were guests as well as ourselves, I'd overheard an exchange. Emily had been asked what she'd thought of the decision to close the school early for the holiday so that the boys would be able to travel home before the sandstorms in the north began: had she been surprised, had she ever heard of such a thing? She'd laughed, then answered matter-of-factly that she hadn't heard the news till a few days later as she and Charles hadn't been speaking to each other at the time. I'd had two thoughts: what a relief to hear that other couples fight. But how impossible, not to speak for an entire day!

Putting my new book away now to get ready for the Christmas dinner, looking again at the cover, at the sketch of the woman staring straight out at me, flanked by a man on either side, I again resolved that I'd begin all over again as soon as I'd come to the end. On second reading I'd proceed more slowly, find the passages that had been the making of what seemed my ungenerous response to Isabel, of which I was a little ashamed.

I remembered my old teacher's telling us that literature was not a tea party; it wasn't to like or dislike characters that we came to great fiction. It was to understand the novel whole, to make out the ways in which each character sheds light on the others, to discover the figure in the carpet, to enter more deeply into what he called the eternal mystery of things. So I tried to forgo judgment.

II

But my rereading of the first half of the novel was delayed a long time. Instead, settled once more during the long afternoons in the sling-backed chair in the blessedly empty days following Christmas, as soon as I'd made my way to the last page, I immediately began to read the second half all over again. I couldn't bear to return to the opening chapters of the book, knowing what lay ahead for Isabel. It was too terrible, her fate, out of all proportion to her failings, and I pitied her deeply. I already knew that the trap had unknowingly been set by Ralph, who himself persuades his dying father to leave a large share of his own inheritance to Isabel, explaining he would like to see her with the "means to meet the requirements of her imagination." But the trap is sprung by another guest staying at Gardencourt during the time of old Daniel Touchett's death. This is Madame Merle, the very model of propriety, of taste and social ease, who immediately sees in Isabel's newly acquired money the vehicle of her own opportunity. She also is American, but who would ever guess? She has lost all her native edges, is "the great round world itself." She never betrays herself; her own past has been swept entirely out of sight. She will introduce Isabel to Gilbert Osmond, yet another American living abroad, but even less a one, if possible, than Madame Merle. Although she describes him as her "friend," in reality he is the father of her unacknowledged child, Pansy. With a little urging Osmond will do the rest. As for Isabel after she inherits her uncle's money—the universe is at her feet. But now her freedom makes her dizzy. What is she to do with herself? Does she look foolish, going around with so much money, so at liberty? Osmond steps into her path. There is something in the picture of this solitary man living with his daughter in a beautiful villa in Florence that arrests her. He is a man of exquisite taste, a collector of art, cosmopolitan. He is low on funds. She marries him. The next we see of her it is more than three years later and she is living in Rome, in the Palazzo Roccanera, "a dark and massive structure," a kind of fortress. We learn almost immediately—but only through the characters surrounding her—that the marriage is unhappy. It is mentioned in passing that she has lost a baby boy, that he died when he was only six months old.

But there was another reason—besides wanting to avoid the horror of watching Isabel cautiously, deliberately, draw close to the trap set for her—that I decided to reenter her story towards the middle of the book, at that point where she has already taken the defining step. I'd encountered very few novels in which marriage played a critical role—or for that matter, in which Americans living abroad did, either—and certainly not during these brief months I'd been married myself that had been spent almost entirely in Nigeria.

Most novels I'd read had ended with a marriage, but the entire second volume of this one was devoted to what happened after the exchange of vows. Some knowledge I blindly felt to be essential was stored in this book. My own marriage was altogether different from Isabel's in that the person I'd married could scarcely have been more unlike

Osmond; full of plans and projects, he was decidedly the "active, larger, freer" type that Ralph Touchett, in trying to warn Isabel before she marries, had imagined would be the sort of man for her. What's more, at Igbobi College I was living in a more complex, a more cosmopolitan world than I'd ever known. The parochial world of my childhood had been swept away. Far from shutting out the wide world, as Isabel's marriage had so miserably done, my own new life had opened a way into it.

The Christmas dinner had been a great success, and in the midst of it I'd thought that far from missing my lost family, I was overjoyed to be among these new people who were so kind to us! That C. and I were newly delighted with each other was the wave that carried me. But during the days that followed—those easy, open, reading days—I knew the wave would inevitably recede, and that we would find ourselves in a more ordinary place where the bottom could once again fall out. How was it, then? My own questions were the ones driving the novel. What did it mean to have chosen someone you'd promised to live with always? What were the forces that had gone into that choice? What fears, what passions? And once married, how did you come to terms with your new knowledge of yourself? Of the other person? Most of all, in the face of this lost innocence, how did you live together from day to day in intimate harmony? And what about that other lost innocence that came with residing outside your own country? I was prepared to read, as Miss Hughes would have said, for my life. In drawing closer to Isabel Archer, I hoped to see more clearly into myself.

Lagos could not have been more unlike Florence or Rome, it seemed, although I'd never visited either one. But obscurely, without in any way spelling out the likeness, I'd already recognized Isabel as a familiar. It may have been this very recognition that set me against her in the first place, the mirror suddenly thrust in my face. There she was, arriving for the first time in England, encased in the light armor of principle, eager to discover and learn, yet determined to protect herself against knowledge. No one was on the scene now to recall her to her former self, to New York, to Albany. I already knew something about that, the blind hope of living beyond the dull particulars of your own past. Living in another place, there was the chance to make yourself up anew, to discard the unwanted, the unflattering. Yet all the time, beneath that air of invulnerability, I also knew the quaver, the fear of being lost in uncertainties and confusion. Even in so brief a time, I recognized Isabel's telling combination of boldness and hesitation, her careening on the edge. I considered my own bumbling entrance into the classroom, my efforts day by day not to act the fool, and blushed.

As someone living outside my own country, I had quickly learned that however much I might want to distance myself from it, I would not be allowed to do so. I was living on the very ground from which some of my students' ancestors, Oridota perhaps, or Binitie—who could tell?—had stepped beneath the weight of chains and shackles into the hold of a ship. Their coerced and anguished labors had amassed the fortune that served as backing for my own privilege and pride. I could alienate myself from this knowledge only at the cost of some irredeemable lie. It wasn't a matter of living inside one's native country or not. It was rather a question of the limits of self-invention.

But I had not yet given much thought to the personal, the deeply personal, aspects of my innocence. I would try to see it as it was reflected in Isabel, a character in a book. I would ponder the fate of a young woman who had married, just as I had, who had felt free when she was not, who had stepped quite deliberately into marriage knowing nothing whatever about what she was doing. Neither had I known anything about what I was doing. Nor did I know much more now. Although I was relatively certain my marriage had not been carefully plotted by others for the sake of their convenience, I knew very little about the web of circumstances that had come into play in what had been called my choice. In some unaccountable way Isabel Archer was unknown to me just as I was unknown to myself. In the case of marriage, reasons counted for little; it was more necessities, urgencies, that dictated.

Just before our departure for Nigeria, the program that was sending us had sponsored a week-long training session to prepare our group of twenty for life in Nigeria. We had gathered mid-August in Elizabethtown, Pennsylvania, not far from the town of Hershey, where one day we were taken on a tour of the chocolate factory and given outsized bars of milk chocolate. But amid lectures on African history and sessions with a nurse who gave us our immunizations as well as the prophylactic, Aralen, that we'd take every week as protection against malaria, we were also each required to spend a half hour with a psychiatrist. He'd been brought in to determine our suitability for living abroad. Almost immediately he asked me what I feared most about living in Nigeria. There seemed many things to say but without thinking much about it I told him it was spiders. I was afraid of spiders. Not the flat kind that skittered across a wall but the ones that were free-standing, that spun a web and then waited in it for passing prey. He told me he thought that what I was afraid of was not the spider but the web, the complicated, shining web. I thought he was wrong about this, told him so. But I was to remember our conversation now.

III

When I dipped back into the second half of *The Portrait of a Lady,* one afternoon a few days after Christmas, I turned to the astonishing chapter 42, in which the reader is invited to listen in on Isabel's solitude, to come as close to her as she is to herself. I remembered that on my first reading, when I reached this point, I had been starved for news of Isabel, the suspense had been acute. The novel had skipped over the scene in which she agrees to Osmond's proposal, as well as the story of the intervening years of her marriage. But at this juncture the narrative takes a sharp turn inward. Isabel, after a walk with Pansy in the Campagna one afternoon, returns to the Palazzo to come upon Madame Merle and Osmond alone together— he sitting in a chair, she standing nearby—lost in a mutual gaze, wordlessly communing. The moment is over almost before it has begun, but Isabel has received an impression: their air of silent intimacy has arrested her. That night, as the candles burn down in their sockets and the clock strikes the small hours and the great, she sits by the dying fire, "her soul . . . haunted with terrors which crowded to the foreground of thought as quickly as a place was made for them," pondering the place she has come to, the inner chambers of the marriage where she now resides. "She could live it over again, the incredulous terror with which she had taken the measure of her dwelling. Between those four walls she had lived ever since; they were to surround her for the rest of her life. It was the house of darkness, of dumbness, of suffocation."

As Isabel's imagination moves freely over these brief years of her marriage that have brought their frightening revelations—her own deep mistrust of her husband; his fury that he has been unable to shape her to his requirements; his hatred of her; his canny hold on himself—she acknowledges the essential nature of the man she has married, a perception altogether lost on her during the time of their courtship. "He took himself so seriously; it was something appalling. Under all his culture, his cleverness, his amenity, under his good nature, his facility, his knowledge of life, his egotism lay hidden like a serpent in a bank of flowers."

The servants bring fresh candles, go to bed, and Isabel sits on, sorting through her early impressions of Osmond, the qualities that had seduced her. She'd considered him the most enlightened of men—the finest, the subtlest, free of all sordid ambition, all narrow prejudice—and it was partly to give him the means he'd lacked that she'd married him. What she had not understood was that under the guise of caring nothing for the world, he cared for nothing else. His eyes were constantly on how the world perceived him. His commanding motive, his supreme wish, was to appear enviable in the eyes of others, to exact a recognition of his own superiority. And it is now in the service of this worship of appearance she is expected to observe his traditions: made-up affairs, rigid codes of behavior, studied attitudes, ingenious forms designed to mystify those on the outside. Indeed, soon after they'd met, he'd told her that he went in for the proprieties, that he was convention itself. But she hadn't understood, she'd read him amiss. "He was not changed; he had not changed; he had not disguised himself, during the year of his courtship, any more than she. But she had seen only half his nature then, as one saw the disk of the moon when it was partly masked by the shadow of the earth. She saw the full moon now—she saw the whole man."

As if reminded of something, I looked up from the page to see the round metallic disk of the sun above the dusty field. It must have been almost four o'clock in the afternoon but at any hour, during the harmattan season, you could gaze at the sun as long as you liked. In the morning the sun came up a deep blood red. In the evening it sank the same. If you'd caught sight of it, then, balanced on the horizon, you couldn't look away: for only a moment it hovered there, immense, shimmering, before sliding rapidly below. Now a black kite, high above the field, drifted back and forth across the disk, swinging round and back, a bird floating on the updrafts, gliding, turning, scanning the field. At any moment it might descend like an arrow to snatch up a bright-headed lizard, a mouse. The afternoon was so still, so silent, that I could hear its high clear whistle, its anguished whinnies. It was Sheila who'd taught me to recognize the kite's call, look for its forked tail. I thought it must be visible floating over the tennis court where, just now, C. was playing a match with Simon. In my mind's eye I could see C. in his white shorts leaping for a shot, hitting the ball at a slant so it dropped just on the other side of the net.

It required a little distance to contemplate my own marriage and I was glad C. was not in a room nearby. I calculated that on the evening of Isabel's vigil by the fire—when she found herself in possession of so clear and terrifying a knowledge of who he was, the man she'd vowed to live with the rest of her years—Isabel must have already been married three years longer than I had. Was less than a year of marriage, then, too brief a time to take any kind of stock? I had no clarity of any kind. In truth, it was the lack of clarity about how things stood that seemed the most glaring fact of my own brief married life. If a full moon was gradually swimming into view, emerging from its earthly shadow, I had no sense of it. Nothing at all was so clearly visible, so distinct. For instance, I thought of C. as much more spontaneous than myself, throwing himself into things where I held back. He was now picking up Yoruba greetings as well as Igbo ones, trying them out on strangers in the market as well as on the schoolboys. He was learning simple sentences in both languages. And he was generous toward people in a way that moved me: he'd told me the other night that he'd offered Umenne help with school fees next year when Umenne was in Moscow studying engineering. When we invited people, C. wholeheartedly threw people together without anxiety as against my worrying whether or not they'd get on well together. On the other hand, he might retire into a preoccupied silence that if I wanted particularly to talk at the time struck me as unfriendly. I didn't know, was beginning to wonder whether reckoning with a certain mystery about the other person was the mark of living intimately with someone; you couldn't always know what they were thinking. Living beside another person, maybe some distance was necessary.

And I remembered how not long ago I'd promised myself, one evening on the balcony, that at some future time I'd record a moment of happiness, the shuffle of C.'s sandal on the wooden steps, his approach. But guessed if I were ever to write such a record he himself would remain in the shadows. If C. and I were to become estranged as Isabel was from Osmond, or separated, or one of us were dead, then a portrait might be possible. The time together would be over. It might seem seductive, then, even compelling, to try to fix in words the person known so intimately. But if C. were *there*—and still perceived as changing in the mysterious ways I perceived myself as changing—I guessed he would elude me as he did now.

Because so far the only constant seemed the changing reality between us. I had trouble recognizing myself, this brand-new married self that was so unpredictable, now one of two rather than one alone. I was more needy of his company than I had ever imagined I'd be, more insecure, more demanding of attention. It seemed I had no sooner stepped out of childhood than I had been thrust back in. Or it might be that he was the one who wanted to spend time together, to talk about a book he was reading, just as I was turning to my own. Nothing was in focus for long. One would suddenly rise to claim something apart from the couple we had become, asserting a separate will, then soon afterwards collapse into the other's arms with happy relief. Yes, we fought at times and were miserable, but it seems we didn't remain angry. Something would always happen to pull us out of it. Our dispute might be pushed aside because a boy we both taught had said something remarkable in class, or a blue aerogramme arrived with news from home, and we'd have to tell the other immediately. We had tender fun. We had names for things. We knew we were very young and we pitied each other, could weigh—each for the other— the burdens implicit in the promises we'd made.

We were each terrified of being controlled, usually overlooking—in the grip of fear—that we were quite willing at some other time to exert our own blind will. Stay with me! It is what I need from you and you must comply! We'd forget the living, the loved face of the other, all we already knew about shared vulnerability and pain. For a moment we'd play the despot, manipulating the other, sometimes subtly, sometimes unashamedly. That there were other ways of dealing with difference we already knew in our hearts but were only beginning to understand; it wasn't necessary to renounce your own ways and tribe in order to cross borders into a new, a common terrain. It was fear that still held us back.

But I was aware that what set Isabel's marriage and mine wholly apart—what made the radical difference—was that I increasingly felt loved for who I was. I might not be able to summon a coherent sense of either C. or myself, but I recognized it was his quick generosity, his intuitive embrace of difference, that allowed me to feel cherished. I would have been ashamed to display the full scope of my rage before even my closest friends. But C. had seen that I could lash out, when frightened. If he'd walked through the door on Christmas Eve, waking me from my unhappy sleep, or returned a little earlier while I was still awake and fuming on the sofa, he would have encountered my unleashed anger, a display of which I would have been miserably ashamed afterwards. It had been the song of the magi on the stairs that had stopped me, the sight of C.'s eager face, holding the gifts.

But had I come undone, C. would not have turned against me. He'd have been hurt, angry. He'd have withdrawn. But in time he'd have given me the benefit of the doubt. As if early on he'd recognized something in my unruly temper essential to who I was, had vowed that our story would not be without a sequel to whatever had pulled us apart. A vow that has become my own and lasted and held.

I remembered how we'd returned along the Ikorodu Road with its lanterns throwing light into the darkness of Christmas Eve, the sense of raw happiness I'd carried within, how we'd fallen into bed as soon as we got home. Our sexual feeling for each other had something to do with our reconciliations, or rather some hidden sympathy asserted itself that expressed itself sexually. However shakily, it seemed to me I was growing in self-assurance. Isabel, on the other hand, had come to believe that Osmond hated her. This had become the one irreducible fact of her marriage, the one that shrouded her days.

But what of Osmond and Isabel, the sexual pull between them? Even though I had several months to wait before I would learn what it was to have a child, I marveled that Isabel's ponderings before the fire at no point touch on the loss of her little son, the baby who died at six months. Early in the second half of the book—at a time when we know nothing whatsoever about Isabel's marriage—this fact is dropped in conversation by Madame Merle and a few pages later again circled round in Ralph's silent ponderings. But it is never alluded to again in all the remaining chapters, and I was haunted by questions. How fiercely, for example, had Isabel mourned her loss? And how had Osmond behaved around the birth and death of this infant, he who is so passionate a father to Pansy? It was easy to forget there had been a child at all. Or perhaps the baby was nothing more than a way of saying that this strange pair had actually met in bed?

Because I couldn't at all make out how things had stood

between Isabel and Osmond during their courtship, couldn't feel what there was between them that had driven it, as in the case of my own marriage. On Isabel's first visit to his villa in Florence, in the company of Madame Merle, Osmond sits in his beautiful room with Pansy standing between his legs—Pansy, fifteen years old, his daughter in her little white dress, waiting for permission to go play in the garden. What could this mean? It was all too strange—even disturbing— and I couldn't understand how Isabel had found this scene compelling. Because what kind of lover had Osmond made at the outset? It was hard to imagine his losing himself in passion after their marriage, hard to imagine this master of irony giving himself over to the study of Isabel's pleasure. Did he shame her? Mock her spontaneities? What I loved was the tenderness at the heart of sexual passion, the nonsense, the silliness. The willingness to make a fool of oneself. C. and I had together read *Goodbye to All That,* and when the narrator writes that after four children and many years he and his wife had said unforgiveable things to each other and had to part, we'd decided that those things could only have been sexual slurs, put-downs. Nothing else would be unforgivable.

And so I read on, considering this passage and then another, free during those leisurely days between Christmas and New Year's to sit in the cool of the harmattan morning as well as the warmer afternoons, looking out on the quiet dusty fields, listening for the black kites' high plaintive cry, the predator's keening. The boys who'd so abruptly disappeared played in and out of my thoughts. I remembered that Abubakar— following Cole's recitation of Act III of *Macbeth*—had one morning called out as Lamikanra entered class late: "How now, my lord. Why do you keep alone?" Perhaps even now, up in Zaria, Abubakar was memorizing parts of Act IV to astonish us all when he returned. Perhaps some students who'd returned to Igbo villages and towns were reflecting on Okonkwo's tragedy, looking at their surroundings with new eyes. They might be interviewing their parents for what they remembered about the arrival of the Europeans, about old customs that had fallen into disuse. I didn't know how, but thought the words they'd read this semester—some of the words—would not leave them entirely, just as I knew I'd never forget Isabel, would continue to see her sitting there alone before the dying fire however long I lived.

IV

At the equator, I discovered, afternoons in December are only a few minutes shorter than in June. The difference was scarcely noticeable at all. The sun rose at almost the same hour all year—about six in the morning—and went down twelve hours later. There were no long gray dawns, no lingering sunsets. The rooster crowed beneath our window before it was light, and then the red sun bounded up, the day had begun.

One morning we'd woken and, hearing Ben below, had begun to get dressed. There was no provocation to lie in bed with so much already going on close by: the shutters downstairs hitting the side of the house, the metallic clink of a handle against a bucket's rim, and from somewhere not far away, the rhythmic thud of a pestle as a woman pounded yam for foofoo. I was sitting on the side of the bed, easing my feet into sandals, C. was standing nearby slowly buttoning a long-sleeved shirt—a blue and white striped one I particularly liked—when he came and sat down on the bed beside me. He'd leaned over to look into my eyes, and instead of meeting his gaze I'd looked away. It was one thing to make love with your body but another to give wholly of yourself with your eyes. I wanted no more intimacy, it was much too costly. That's how I'd felt at that instant, but was immediately sorry, was afraid I'd done something hurtful to C., to myself. All this took place in no more than a second, no words were spoken. But I knew I'd remember it. Before I could try to mend things, C. had stood up and finished buttoning his shirt, the moment had passed. Then we were on our way down the stairs for breakfast.

Later on that same day, walking slowly up the stairs, noticing the dust that now filmed the leaves of the vine winding round the bannister, it occurred to me that my fear of being left alone was sparked not by what I thought of as C.'s occasional distance but by my own ambivalence about the demanding life of intimacy I'd embarked on. For why had I refused to meet C.'s gaze? And so, I decided, in trying to look more closely at Isabel's secret motives for marrying Osmond, I'd try to get closer to the forces that had driven me.

During her lonely vigil Isabel had given a long look to the dark side of Osmond's moon. But what, I thought, about the obscure side of her own? What that was frail and self-doubting in herself had led her to choose Osmond?

Because there was something pitiably narrow in Isabel too, at this juncture. It's not only her inexperience, her innocence, that keeps her from perceiving what is sinister in Osmond. It's her own high sense of privilege that blocks the light, the very quality that had made her less than sympathetic in the first half of the book. It seemed there was something sealed off in her, a closed door that prevents her from intuiting that Madame Merle is lacking in naturalness. Or that Osmond dwells in the regions of ice. Why is Isabel impervious to what others recognize as pose, as studied effect? Entirely deracinated, citizens of nowhere, Osmond and Madame Merle have no roots, no responsibilities, no scruples, no loyalties. They confess to no shame, no embarrassment. If they are to make use of the world, they must not give themselves away, must appear irreproachable, beyond blame. Who knows who they are? What they are? Where they come from?

Isabel, who is used to being generally admired—indeed regarded by everyone as a superior being—is concerned for the impression she is making on Osmond when Madame Merle takes her for the first time to his villa. Afraid of saying the wrong thing, she dreads exposing "a possible grossness of perception." It's his sensibility that attracts her, mystifies: the sharp edge of his irony that she has not yet experienced as cutting. Because even during their courtship, he will humiliate her. It is what he does so well, gives out an air that subtly demeans. She fears looking ridiculous in his eyes, going about the world with so much money in her pocket. She tells him he knows everything and she knows nothing and he answers gravely that he doesn't know everything. She doesn't perceive the oddness of his making this point.

Is his reserve a version of disgust that she wishes to overcome? Does he want to humiliate her bright sense of superiority? One thing seems certain: in proportion to her own wounded vanity, she is caught. His hidden judgments make her trip. He has not pressed her, he'd let her come to him of her own will. Perhaps, I thought, this is the shining web that attracted her, the sense that he could do without her. To give herself at someone's urgent bidding would be to forfeit her liberty. It was her self-love, after all, the idea she cherishes of her own distinction, that she doesn't see, and what she doesn't see will be the agent of her sorrow. Here I thought of *Wuthering Heights*, of poor Catherine Earnshaw, also used to being generally admired, who out of self-love and a vain fancy to fill the role of first lady of the neighborhood turns away from Heathcliff, her partner in rebellion, and loses her life. And of Nelly Dean, who warns her.

I tried to think what it was I hadn't been aware of that had gone into my own choice. What was the shining web I was afraid of and that I'd failed to see? These were the questions the book had raised.

I was beginning to think about precisely those qualities in myself that were too near to get hold of, too intimate to have any thoughts about. In the clear light of day they were imperceptible, at nighttime they appeared only in dreams. These were the necessities, the urgencies, perhaps the accidents of self, that had shaped me up until now and would certainly play a part in my future. My meditations on Isabel—giving me a sharpened sense of the self-love that might accompany innocence—matched my new understanding of the benighted sense of high privilege, bred in the bone, I'd carried with me from home. The vanities to which I clung, the pride for which I excused myself too easily. And here I suddenly wondered if one kind of innocence, at least, was vanity by another name, a willful hiding from yourself and your intimates, eyes averted at the last moment.

Before me were whole stretches, still, of the shadowed side of my own moon that had not yet swung into view. I didn't know much about all that, but the book told me I must be on the alert, at least, for what I didn't see. It's the things we don't know about in ourselves, I thought, that blind us, lead us straight into suffering. Yet was it only life itself that could show us these spots of blindness? And if so, was suffering inescapable?

V

Not so long ago I'd been afraid of living wholly inside of books. Fear of the unlived life had propelled me out of them. Reading, I'd thought, was a substitute for living, a sphere apart in which the reader underwent the characters' lives rather than her own. Instead, I would take my chances. I'd belong in an ordinary way to the world of human beings, with its inevitable burden of pain and sorrow. Life will not spare you, boys and girls, Miss Hughes had told us. It spares no one.

And yet here I was, sitting on the verandah with the book resting on my belly where I'd begun to feel a slight mound, looking out at frangipani leaves now coated with dust, pondering Isabel's life as a way of pondering my own. What could this mean? It was as if I needed a novel, after all, to decipher events. Life was too fluid to reflect on, too transient. One state of feelings replaces another too quickly. If I hadn't known this already, the past few days had made clear to me the shifting nature of truth as judged in the light of feeling. But in the pages of a novel, time is slowed down so that you can feel within yourself what is transpiring. You can stop, you can ponder. And then see. In reading, you can find yourself where you are. Had I been mistaken, then, to think that reading must lead me away from life rather than toward it?

I read more and more slowly, moving for the second time toward the end of the book, following Isabel to Gardencourt to sit beside the dying Ralph, to receive Caspar Goodwood's passionate kiss, and then, finally, to return alone—where we cannot follow her—to Rome. What is to become of her? Will she leave Osmond, once Pansy is provided for? She is now armed with the knowledge of Osmond's deception and wouldn't he therefore be forced to approach her differently?

Or, indeed, would he not. Because anything is possible with Osmond. It is he who strikes the note of terror in the book, the character who turns it into a horror story: the tale of a beautiful young woman who finds herself in the dark with a murderous stranger she had trusted. A danger implicit in any marriage, perhaps, but here the possibility opens to its most intimate flowering. Osmond is ego on the prowl, he is the uncanny force of evil, poised to seize and control. His intention is to colonize Isabel, to take to himself her considerable resources so as to increase his position in the world. He will fit her to his purposes. Like the devil, he has his reasons, ones that have the familiar ring of pieties. If violence is done, it is accomplished in the quietest possible fashion, the whip well hidden behind the elaborately worked tapestry.

And so Isabel is made to suffer, and in her suffering she is humbled, is made kind. Her self-assurance is transformed into imagination for the sufferings of others that had seemed so lacking the night of her arrival in Gardencourt. The defenseless Pansy has become her tender charge.

I closed the book watching a thin trail of blue smoke rise from the farthest end of the field. Tomorrow would be New Year's Day. I would read this book again, at some later time, and perhaps I would understand its characters differently. Perhaps, in years to come, when I'd lived a little longer, I'd be able to follow Isabel out of the book. But for the moment, her inner life had given me something of what I so desperately needed, a way into my own. It was very odd but it seemed to me that, different as our two experiences had been, Isabel had become my confidante, my sister. I knew I hadn't been transformed by the suffering of others but could see that if I allowed for that possibility, there might be opportunities.

And yet, I thought uneasily, I couldn't put the book away quite yet. Wasn't there something even now, some further recognition, that lay concealed in its pages? Some leap of the imagination I'd been reluctant to make? I thought there might be some glimpse of my own dark side I'd turned away from, not unlike the one Badagry had revealed, that blow to my national pride. But in this case a more intimate pride, my own.

Because much as I wanted to see Osmond as the most irredeemable of creatures, as a predator belonging not to the human but to the animal world, I was beginning to see that, repugnant as the thought might be, he recalled me to myself. Did he not embody at its most terrifying the urge I had become familiar with these past months? The need to regulate things, to order them to my own liking? Yes, even in so short a time, I had been struck by the fact that marriage involved subtle coercions, manipulations, involved the desire—sometimes the overwhelming need—to bend another's will to the requirements of one's own. Stay with me! Do as I wish! Indeed, someone else's ideas were always the difficulty, as they had been for Osmond. They stood in the way.

We had arrived in Africa, as in marriage, with a conviction of our own virtue that had served for a while. But we were beginning to learn. We had begun to see into ourselves and the country we called ours. It was the simplest thing in the world to make use of another person. And to find quite benevolent reasons for doing so. The world would not object. I could already see it would be a life's work, renouncing the impulse to control. To resist playing the tyrant in the face of one's own devouring need. I'd learned, too, that if I allowed my own demands full rein—as on Christmas Eve—the door would swing open to suffering.

And I was beginning to make out that the solitary self, the person I was when alone and reading and dreaming, would never find its truest expression, of which I could foresee so little, without the labors of loving. The world was opening before me. In C.'s dark eyes I would sometimes glimpse the vulnerabilities that my will had struggled to override. I would like to have made little of any obstacle that stood in my way but now was sometimes stopped by the sharp apprehension that it was in my power to wound.

VI

The next day we were taking the train to the north, to Hausaland. We were traveling to Kano. An American couple who had also come to Nigeria with Teachers for West Africa had visited us in the last weeks and urged us to return the visit. Kano was entirely different from Lagos, they told us. They'd take us to the camel market, we'd eat dates, drink mint tea in little glasses. We'd hear the call to prayer from a nearby mosque, observe people all around us touching their foreheads to the ground in prayer. In the afternoon we'd see old men in black turbans sitting on their mats, fingering their beads. Hausa was altogether different from the languages of the coast; we'd find it easier to speak. It wasn't hard at all to learn the greetings. But on the train we must be careful to keep the windows closed to prevent coal specks from flying in!

I wanted to travel to the north but I didn't want to put the book away, even though I knew I'd find it waiting for me when we returned in a couple of weeks. I didn't want to leave Ben, either, or the dusty vines climbing the stairs. The year was ending. A new one was about to begin. That border in time would be crossed as surely as the one we'd crossed when we'd come to live in Nigeria. As surely, for that matter, as the one we'd crossed when we'd married.

I imagined our train racing northward along silver tracks bordered by dense rain forest that gave way bit by bit to dry savannah. I had a picture of savannah but in truth had never seen it or the people living in it. And then—feeling my way toward an analogy that was only half-glimpsed, felt rather than known—I asked myself if marriage was like travel, like living in another country where you didn't know the terrain. You might have ideas about the country, have ideas about yourself in that country, but as these fall away something else emerges. You're still a citizen of your own country, all the life you've lived up to that time. But now new and unusual customs surround you, food and manners, ways of being in the world, silences and talk, kindnesses and tyrannies, shames and confusions and sudden freedoms, vistas and confined places. These are now part of the air you breathe. And in inhabiting another place, the land that was your own doesn't look the same anymore. Your identity, the citizenship you'd taken for granted, changes as you cross borders. You will never be able to return as an innocent. And that's because once you've glimpsed that another person is no less vulnerable to hurt than yourself, no less hopeful of good or fearful of injury, some of your own complicities become clear. As, indeed, do your vanities, your need to be praised and admired that make so little of the vivid ache and longings of the other. But at the same time, it seemed, illuminations might flash like lightning across a blind sky. There were the unbidden, the heart-stopping gifts that when least expected arrived on your doorstep.

The harmattan was blowing and our friends in Kano had said that in the north nights were cooler than in Lagos: we'd need to sleep beneath blankets purchased in the market. In the morning we'd walk around the crumbling walls of the ancient city, count off each of its fourteen gates. Who knows, perhaps we'd even travel north and cross the border into Niger, see the blue-robed Tuaregs moving silently on their white camels across the sand. Speak French, go for a dinner of *biftek* and *frites* in the open court of the Hôtel Central in Zinder, talk late under a sky brilliant with stars. There was an abandoned French fort on the hill we could visit the next morning where troops had been garrisoned, huge gray boulders tumbling beneath its ramparts in casual disarray.

And beyond, waiting for us that day or another, just as it happened, one year or the next, the open desert where under a reeling sun we would find or lose our souls.

Madame Bovary

I

Facts: Avesnes-sur-Helpe is a town in the north of France, a little west of the Ardennes, and only fourteen kilometers from the Belgian border. The river Helpe Majeure, a tributary of the Sambre, flows through the town. Because of its strategic location on the road running from Brussels to Paris, Avesnes was chosen as the German headquarters for the Western Front and it was from here that Wilhelm II and Hindenburg directed the last German offensive in 1918. A century earlier, Napoleon had delivered his own final directives, on the eve of the battle of Waterloo, from the rectory of Saint-Nicolas, the town's fourteenth-century church. And more than a century before that, during the wars of expansion of Louis XIV, Avesnes was one of several cities in the region fortified by Vauban; in a footnote the guidebook adds that beneath its skies that same Louis had first enjoyed the favors of Montespan.

These were some of the things we learned during the brief year we spent in Avesnes, teaching English at the Institut Ste.-Thérèse, a *pensionnat* where the daughters of prosperous farmers and tradespeople came to finish their schooling or prepare for the baccalaureate. Our two years in Nigeria at Igbobi College had passed too quickly and we had left Africa sorrowfully, vowing to return. We had only vague plans for the future but were sure we didn't want to plunge back into life at home. At twenty-five, we thought it too soon to put an end to our travels. We had two little girls now, one a year and a half old and the other an infant; we referred to them as "the babies" and didn't see why they shouldn't begin seeing the world in their infancy, as we had not. And there may have been another reason: the war in Vietnam was heating up and, although we wouldn't have put it this way, we may have thought we could escape national responsibility by staying out of the country. A flurry of applications for teaching positions in France had produced nothing and it seemed we'd have to return after all. When, at the last minute, the Institut Ste.-Thérèse offered jobs beginning in the fall of 1965, we jumped to accept. We knew nothing of this region of France—or any other region for that matter—and in preparation began reading novels by French writers, thinking that would at least be something.

The convent to which the Institut was attached gave us a stone farmhouse to live in that belonged to one of its sisters, Soeur Marie Joliette. The house was located two miles out from Avesnes, on the route de Landrecies, and parts of it were already occupied by M and Mme Druet, who looked after the farm and its twenty cows. Two rooms were made available to us: one upstairs where we all slept, one down. The salon upstairs with its chairs covered in red velvet and the bedroom furnished with bamboo furniture were off-limits. Built flush up against the Route de Landrecies, the house had a pebbled margin in front just wide enough for the van that brought Mme Druet's *baguettes* on Sunday to sweep through and out. Across the road, sloping down and away, rich pastures descended to the village of Saint-Hilaire, where a steeple was visible on clear days from the room upstairs. Clear days, though, were the exception: on the first day of November the cows drifted across the road and into the barn, where they remained for a winter of drizzle and fog.

At the side of the house, down a few scant steps from the kitchen, spread a neglected garden of yellow chrysanthemums, scrappy in the September sun, Michaelmas daisies, and something called *joli bois* that edged the path leading down to the coal bin. Sitting on the steps in the early afternoon, I could watch the flies make their heavy way back and forth from flower to kitchen, droning in the heat, pausing to alight on a wedge of Maroilles cheese abandoned on a plate beside the shallow sink, or hovering a moment above the fading leaves of the strawberry patch. This patch, when in bloom the following spring, would provoke a warning: the fruit, we were told by Soeur Marie Joliette—who had been a child in this house, whose father had died only the year before in a room upstairs—was intended for the convent. It was Soeur Marie Joliette who on the day of our arrival had pronounced our little girl *sauvage*, even as I held her in my arms while introductions were being made. Wild! The poor child was clearly taken aback by this woman she'd never met who seemed so self-assured. It was only later on that evening, looking up the word in the little dictionary we carried everywhere, I understood that "sauvage" in French means timid. And immediately thought of a deer startling away.

In the evenings, as the autumn wore on, M and Mme Druet sometimes invited us into their kitchen in back for a *tasse de café*, a cup holding a potent blend of chicory made from the roots of the blue meadow flower that at twilight closes to a pale lavender. This would be after the babies were settled for the night, the door left ajar so we could listen for them. Next to the entry leading out to the barn where the cows breathed into the chilly air, M Druet's wooden *sabots* stood side by side with Pierre's, muddy from the damp soil and manure of the courtyard. Pierre was the elder son who had returned from the Algerian war and was for the moment helping his father. He was usually watching television in a room off the kitchen when we entered but always stood tall and lean in the doorway a minute or two and wished us a good evening. M Druet, sitting there at the table in silence, lifting his cup to his lips and setting it down, wore gray felt slippers exactly like the ones we'd found upstairs in the armoire, left behind by the dead man, Soeur Marie Joliette's father.

It was Madame, having taken off her blue smock for company and hung it on a hook by the door, who did the talking. No, they'd never made the three hours' journey to Paris; the cows, we must know, had to be milked, morning and night. The farthest away either of them had been from Avesnes, where they'd both been born, was Verdun, where Monsieur had fought in 1916. He'd been scarcely older at the time than their younger son Patrick, fifteen years old, who sat with us at the table and whose massive shoulders shook now and then with suppressed laughter at something his mother said. As for herself, she continued, raising a hand, pursing her lips, well, this had been her life. After all, they hadn't needed to go anywhere to see the Germans march by twice on the route de Landrecies, at an interval of twenty-five years. Of course they hadn't lived in the house at that time, it wasn't till afterwards. But Soeur Marie Joliette's father, poor man, who had been born within these walls, had been forced to leave for some months: the house had been conscripted by a German general, who slept in the bed upstairs.

That would be our bed, the one that sloped in at the middle, where the German general's weight had sagged, and where we now woke to the bells of Saint-Hilaire if the babies hadn't woken us earlier. While the general snored, his leather boots may have stood side by side in the armoire. It was empty now except for the abandoned slippers and what looked like a copper vase, burnished and tall, standing upright in a corner. That was *un obus*, Soeur Marie Joliette had told us, a shell casing that had once contained explosives and been turned up by a plow in the outlying fields. These could be found all over the neighborhood, shined up, and put to use in summer to hold Queen Anne's lace, cornflowers, and daisies.

It was the storeroom below that was crowded with objects. In a corner of the dining room that served also as sitting room—and where, on the mantel, a large bust of Christ presided that looked as if it had been modeled on Bernini's *Louis Quatorze*—two steps led up to a door that opened onto a shadowy alcove dim with cobwebs and looming confusion. Too low to stand up in, this little storeroom bulged with things once chosen by men and women now dead: a shovel, tongs, and bellows black from use in the fireplace presently occupied by a porcelain stove, a *poêle*, which we fed with coal; little shades for candles; a traveling trunk with an iron hasp; a tin bathing tub with a tall back to lean against; a bouquet of dried flowers tied with a ribbon; a milky shaving glass; gilt candlesticks; carved wooden eggcups; and a bandbox empty of collars.

Whose were these and where had they come from? Soeur Marie Joliette's father had not lived far away enough in time. And the German general didn't enter into it; these were not the objects he had handled and lived among. Or if he had, they would only reluctantly have been touched by his fingers. They had given themselves to someone else entirely. My head was already full of the books I'd been reading as a preparation for this stay in France so it didn't take a minute to think of Emma Bovary. These objects might well have belonged to her, to Yonville-l'Abbaye, the scene of her torment. Here in the dim storeroom were things that might have soothed her hungry senses, the mirror her eyes had looked into, the footstool covered in red satin on which she had rested her feet before the fire, the tub where she had sat naked and despaired that the exaltations of her spirit would ever find a lover worthy of them.

Of course this was Avesnes-sur-Helpe, *sous-prefecture* of *le Nord*, closer to the Ardennes than to Normandy. But a market town, all the same, like Yonville, where farmers set up stalls in the Place du General Leclerc at the foot of Saint-Nicolas to sell cheeses, wines, rabbits and pheasants, farm gear and seed, dresses and sweaters and shoes. A *place* like that at Yonville, where the agricultural show had been punctuated by Rodolphe's seduction of Emma, where she had looked at him as at a voyager who has traveled in many lands, catching on his beard the scent of vanilla and citron. And a countryside all around of pastures and orchards and woods where it was easy to imagine Emma riding out by Rodolphe's side one smoky afternoon in October or running through the meadows before dawn to enter her sleeping lover's room with dewdrops hanging in her black hair.

In fact, there was nothing strange—on that first glimpse into the cluttered depths of the storeroom—in having thought right away of Emma Bovary. As we left Paris one afternoon in early

September and drove north along the *Route nationale* that gave us a glimpse from below of stone oxen looking out from the towers of the hilltop cathedral of Laon, it had been Emma who had begun to stir somewhere on the edges of consciousness. Three hours was the time we had set aside to drive the 200 kilometers to Avesnes. But as the twilight deepened, our spirits faltered. The towns looked more and more dreary, their streets deserted. In Nigeria, just outside the Igbobi compound, on the Ikorodu Road, there had always been people in the streets, moving from one place to another, women carrying babies on their backs, calling out greetings as they passed, stopping to talk or to buy a mango or papaya. Young men strolling out in freshly creased trousers, little girls in school uniforms. In the evenings the streets were lit by oil lanterns beaming hospitably from roadside stands selling cigarettes, cones of salt wrapped in blue paper, scented bars of soap.

In the towns we were passing through now the doors of the houses lining the main streets were shut and the windows hung with lace curtains. There was almost always a memorial to those lost in the First World War in the form of a cross with the names of the dead engraved on it. Then there was the *pharmacie* with its green cross, the *charcuterie*, the *boucherie chevaline* with the signature head of a horse hanging in front of it. In the window of every café a sign advertised the beer of the region: Stella Artois. The only people out and about seemed to be an occasional woman hurrying home with a baguette sticking up from a net bag or a boy disappearing around a corner on his bicycle. Once or twice we saw some old men wearing berets playing *boules* in a ring of dust. Even the poplars retreating down the side streets looked lonely. How would we fare in a town like one of these? I thought of Emma and her futile efforts to find peace, a release from ennui, the harrowing sense that life was escaping her.

Throughout the year in Avesnes, the storeroom never failed to summon the disturbing presence of Emma. It was like a little museum of Yonville confirming that the world Emma had lived in was close enough to touch, the little traveling trunk with the hasp, for instance, probably much like the one she'd ordered from Lheureux when she'd been rapturously dreaming of an elopement with Rodolphe. And there were odd moments, now and then, when suddenly and unexpectedly Emma's plight came vividly alive.

As we had done at Igbobi, after the birth of the babies, C. and I taught alternately during the year in Avesnes, each taking a turn at home. He taught in the mornings, I in the afternoons. Although we had been warned on every side that our lives would become more complex, more demanding after the birth of children, we had found that the presence of the babies set us right. We struggled less about who decided what and discovered common cause in our new purpose. And perhaps our isolation, our sense of estrangement from the place we found ourselves, led us to rely more deeply on each other. We were the sole English speakers in Avesnes, we discovered, and because our French was at first so halting, our only real conversations were with each other. I had never been more grateful for C.'s enlivening energy, the imagination that had carried us to Africa. Now here in Avesnes he proposed outings: that we drive up to Brussels for a Sunday afternoon and eat *moules* and *frites* in a café, that we travel to Antwerp to visit some friends he'd made on a train when he was backpacking in Europe the summer before we'd met. We had an unspoken pact that we would not invoke the babies regretfully as a reason for not doing something, a pact surprisingly easy to keep, once we got the hang of it; a weekend by ourselves in Paris was clearly impossible but we avoided saying isn't it too bad we can't visit the city alone. On the other hand, we planned excursions with the babies we might not have if someone else had been there to look after them.

But there were times when—perhaps because I was nursing our little one, perhaps because in Nigeria C. had handled this kind of thing more than I—he was the one to undertake some common business that involved hours of waiting around an office to fulfill a bureaucratic requirement while I stayed at home alone with the babies. It was during those long housebound days, when the hours seemed to spin endlessly and I felt the bitter loss of friends and our Nigerian students, that I looked around and remembered Emma.

One rainy morning in late October when there was a biting chill in the air and the newly lighted coal stove in the room downstairs gave off more smoke than heat, her presence became frighteningly vivid. Taking advantage of a school holiday, C. had set off early for Lille, *prefecture du Nord*, to secure our *cartes d'identité*. Every day we washed the dirty clothes and diapers in a bucket just as Ben had done— the nearest laundromat was in Mons, across the border in Belgium—and hung them to dry on two lines nailed to solid beams in the attic. This room at the top had sloping wooden ceilings and a low window on one side that looked below onto the route de Landrecies. Today, reluctant as always to leave the babies alone downstairs, I made my laborious way with them and the laundry up the two flights of stairs, stopping on each step. Once in the attic, hastily flinging the wet clothes over the lines, fearful in this shadowy space that the babies might fall down the stairs or tumble into a corner that hid a rusty nail, I took note of the dim dirty light of a rainy day coming in through the window. It fell on the wooden planks of the floor, illuminating a handful of dust, scrappings of mice, a floating cobweb. Immediately I remembered Emma's desperate flight to the top of the house in an attic like this one where she could finally be alone to read Rodolphe's letter of farewell. I remembered with a shiver how she'd looked down into the square below and how the sunlight glinting on the flags had seemed to invite her to leap, to surrender herself to the open blue spaces, and how she'd almost fainted with terror afterwards when she realized how narrowly she'd escaped death.

We made our slow, careful way back down the stairs and ate a lunch of *petits suisses* and hot carrots and potatoes, mashed with butter and salt. Then, while the babies briefly napped, I threw open the windows to clear the room of smoke and ran outside with the scuttle to carry in more coal to feed the fire. Cold rain was falling on the fields and thick hedges, on three black and white cows standing patiently beneath a tree. Across the road in the direction of Saint-Hilaire white smoke drifted across the shiny slate roofs of cottages almost buried in deep grass. Inside again, I sat down at the table and considered correcting student homework, or *devoirs,* as I'd learned to call it. The fire wouldn't quite catch, even with the help of the bellows, and I wanted to rescue the day. Time was spilling, losing itself like water in sand, vanishing in one chore after another. All with an end to keeping us in clean clothes and fed. And more or less warm. Soon it would be time to think of dinner: I'd have to come up with something. The year had barely begun and already I was wishing that anything, anything at all, might happen to break the monotony of the days. This was not at all the life I'd had in mind when we talked about "a year in France." I'd imagined a stone village in Provence, fields of lavender scenting the air, or a cottage in the Loire valley not far from Paris where Miss Hughes had been tempted to despair on the Pont des Arts and where Mozart's *Requiem* had been played at Chopin's funeral in the Madeleine. I thought of people even now in Paris living unknown and adventurous lives, perhaps behind closed shutters, in a room like the one in *À bout de souffle* where Jean Paul Belmondo sat on a bed and traced his upper lip with his thumb.

Then the babies were awake again. After I'd changed them and we all were downstairs I sat on the floor as they played about, the baby teething and wailing into the damp air, the toddler restless from being confined. I gave the baby a wooden spoon to chew on, then sent a big red ball spinning along the floor to our little girl, back and forth between us. Afterward I sang them the songs I was learning in French, *Le petit lapin a du chagrin; il ne saute plus dans le jardin. Sur le pont d'Avignon, on y danse, on y danse.* Each song had hand gestures to go with it, and for a time they were amused. Then, when I'd exhausted my repertory, I made up stories to go with the pictures in a little book bought in Lagos, in Kingsway, about the adventures of Downy Duckling, who falls into an icy pond and who, to the amazement of all the other animals, comes spluttering up at the end.

But nothing, really, was of any use. It was I who was distracted, at odds. C. would not be back for some time and I was wondering how I'd get through the long hours ahead. I found myself sharply resenting his absence. I wondered why it should happen that he was out and about while I was stuck in this smoky room with our crying children. I knew we'd agreed that he would set off alone—one of us had to go—and that I would stay with the babies today, but now I couldn't understand why things should be this way. Was it because I was the woman and nursing? Was it because I was secretly intimidated by the job at hand, that I feared not quite catching something said to me, some essential requirement in France, and so would be unable to secure the IDs and the child benefits that came with them? C. was less hesitant to speak French than I. He plunged ahead, unafraid of making mistakes, asking people to correct him as he went. For the most part he expected to understand, and did. He regarded a new language as an opportunity rather than a barrier. He would represent us better than I could.

Tomorrow, I knew, I'd be in the classroom again and our ordinary life would resume and this day would have safely taken its place in the past. But the next time there was an errand of this kind, I determined, we'd all go together. I feared we were taking on the traditional roles that up till now we'd avoided. It might happen, little by little, that we'd find ourselves swallowed up, separated in lives that had little to do with each other.

Thinking to distract the babies, to distract myself, I flicked on the button of the old-fashioned radio that sat on a ledge beside the door. C. and I sometimes tried to listen in the evenings, but most of the time we weren't able to follow the rapid idiomatic French and I ended up wanting to turn it off. C. argued that we were becoming accustomed to the rhythms of the language even if we couldn't make out much more than individual words. I found it easier when face-to-face with someone, like Mme Druet, who spoke slowly and carefully so that we would understand. We knew her French would be called patois by many, but her kindly eyes made it easy to confess not having understood, and she would patiently begin again, apparently not minding at all. "C'en fait rien du tout!" she'd exclaim, making nothing of our difficulties.

This time, though, with the turn of the button on the radio, into the room swept the sound of Paul McCartney's voice singing "Michelle, ma belle." The song was new and I listened raptly, my thoughts returning to Paris. I dreamt of bistros where people sat in the soft twilight drinking the new autumn Beaujolais, singing the words I quickly learned and now sang aloud: *Sont les mots qui vont très bien ensemble, très bien ensemble.*

Out of nowhere, then, in what seemed an answer to prayer, there came a knock at the door. It was Patrick. He stood shyly in the doorway, silent. I waited a moment, holding the baby on my hip, and asked if he'd like to come in. He answered no, he wouldn't be able to. Again he was silent. Then he said he'd come to ask if it would amuse me to join them, they were about to kill the pig. I looked at him incredulously, wondering if I had understood. How could he have imagined I'd want to witness such a thing! At last I mumbled something about not being able to leave the babies and he'd gone sadly away.

Half an hour later, slicing mushrooms to put in a soup for dinner, I surprised myself by suddenly snorting with laughter. What an extraordinary moment! Who would have imagined!

And yet that night, falling asleep beside a sleeping C.—after his return from Lille with lively stories of the day, after my relating the story of Patrick's invitation and my fear I'd hurt his feelings, after C.'s reassurance that tomorrow we'd make a point of asking him in for coffee—I still worried a little. Patrick had meant only to be kind. Would his offer have seemed less bleak, less desperate, if I had not already been thinking that day of Emma Bovary, if I had not learned to see and feel things at moments like these as Flaubert determined that Emma must? And so shut out the rest of the world? Her isolation had been terrible!

In the end Emma made only chance appearances in Avesnes. "It was the fault of fate," Charles pronounces, after her death, speaking to Rodolphe, unknowingly using the same phrase Rodolphe himself had cynically thrown in when he was composing his goodbye letter to Emma. And so it would have seemed. She didn't exist except as a creature driven by wandering desires that would lead to her own self-destruction. Fate had placed her in Yonville, she belonged to it. She was not passing through. And no one knew this better than Emma, herself, whose own impassioned reading had supplied her with visions of exotic foreign lands she would never visit: Walter Scott's moors and ruins, the little seaside bamboo house of *Paul et Virginie*, the ruddy sunsets and minarets described in the books of her school days. The closest she ever came to translating her dreams into an address, perhaps, was in her fevered fantasies of the aborted elopement with Rodolphe: the gondolas and hammocks, the guitars and fountains, and finally the fishing village where they would live always beneath wide starry skies.

I was not of Avesnes as Emma was of Yonville. My own imagined foreign land had disappointingly been transformed into a town something like her own inescapable home. For the moment, however, my fate had to be worked out in a place that reminded me of hers. And as Emma was destined to be a woman whose struggles had never yielded the least chance against the forces of destruction, who was devastatingly

alone, unconnected by ties of affection to a single child or
school friend or husband or neighbor, she seemed less and
less a guest I wished to entertain. For hadn't Patrick been
meaning—perhaps at the urgings of his mother, who was
aware I was alone—to spare my solitude? I did not choose to
be one of those Bovarys whom Flaubert had remarked were
suffering and crying at that very instant in twenty villages
in France. I did not! As the months went by Emma came
to seem not so much a living presence as a tender memory:
poised, on her own arrival at Yonville, before the chimney
at the *Lion d'Or*, the tips of her fingers catching her dress
at the knee, her foot in its black boot held out to the fire, a
red glow passing over her skin as the wind blew in through
the half-open door.

II

If Emma introduced herself even before we reached
Avesnes, there was another figure who remained elusive,
who for a long while stayed hidden behind a question. But
even the question seemed more a kind of inner prompting,
a restless effort to recall, than a question I could formulate
with any precision. What was it, sitting on the steps above
the chrysanthemums during those first weeks in Avesnes,
homesick for Africa, homesick for I scarcely knew what,
that made me think I'd known it all before, this brooding
midday, the flies adrift around this lump of sugar dunked
in coffee? As if this were my earliest place, this house, these
rooms at my back with their lace curtains, as if my oldest
memories had sprung from this wall of old stones warmed
by the sun, this soft haze of lavender daisies? As if long ago

I had lived and died in this spot and were now being called back, urgently but silently, to a self that, unrestored, I must mourn forever.

There would be other times, too, when it seemed some forgotten past stirred within, a sensation that the present was only a cover for a moment infinitely nearer and more profound. This might happen, for example, during the first period after lunch in a classroom at the Institut Ste.-Thérèse when, its windows open to the steeple of Saint-Nicolas rising close beside us in the *place* outside, the carillon's shower of bells suddenly filled the room—a moment prolonged while the girls sitting at their desks kept silent, as if by solemn agreement, waiting for the wheeze that like a long indrawn breath prepared us for the single great bong announcing the hour.

But it wasn't until one Thursday afternoon in mid-November, when we'd taken advantage of the half holiday to drive to Amiens in order to visit the cathedral—to give us all a change of scene: our little girl the chance to run unhindered up and down the long aisles while we took turns holding the little one, inhaling her downy head, her baby fragrance—that some associations began to gather and hold. The day had begun with fog swirling up against the windowpanes, with C. teaching early morning classes. By the time he'd returned, the sun had begun to come out, the babies were fed. Unpacking the items he'd bought in the market—a baguette, a wedge of Port-Salut, some pâté de campagne, petits suisses, some brussels sprouts—he made a proposal. We'd eat the baguette and paté right away, then put the babies in the back of the car hoping they'd nap on the drive over to Amiens.

They were both asleep by the time we'd driven thirty-two kilometers west along the route de Landrecies, passing through the village of Maroilles and then Landrecies itself to Le Cateau. It was in this gray city, we'd learned, that Matisse had been born and it was from here he had set out on a journey that would take him to Ajaccio, Morocco, and Tahiti before bringing him finally to windows open on an azure sea where in a pool of light a goldfish circled a bowl. I was thinking of all this, of the strangeness of beginnings, when, in the center of Le Cateau, at a crossroads, we passed a sign marked for Cambrai: twenty-two kilometers. I said the name aloud, but tentatively, uncertain about the pronunciation of vowels, when suddenly, rising it seemed from nowhere, an unbidden air of delight seemed to hang in the afternoon. But it was only later—after I'd had time to look around at the slender springing columns that held aloft the vast cathedral, felt the initial surge of joy lift and soar between gleaming walls of light, the promise of eternity float in the high dim spaces— that I finally understood. The murmur of Proust's novel, the long cadences of its lines, had, from our first moments in Paris, without my even knowing it, been running like a current through all my days and nights: *Combray.*

In the weeks following that day at Amiens, I was less and less frequently visited by those premonitions of a reality hovering just beyond reach, on the sunlit brink of discovery. Was it because habit, both bane and blessing, that great anesthetizer, as the narrator of *À La Recherche du Temps Perdu* calls it, was already making familiar and invisible a world that so short a time ago had seemed to promise a life deeply awaited and longed for? Or was it rather that, if I had ever hoped, however unknowingly, to enter Proust's world by coming to live in France, to step live into the landscape he had summoned word by word with so much patience, my expectations were bound to be disappointed? Like the boy in Combray—on a hot summer day stretched on his bed reading while the flies droned about him, inspired by his book with a longing for a land of mountains and rivers, of currents heavy with watercress—I had not understood that the self lost in the pages of a book is the same self we take with us on our travels; that we invest a place, like a person, with a spiritual glamour that is bound eventually to be shown for what it is: a product of our own illusions.

It is only those journeys undertaken from within, the inspired attention to the urgings of our own lost selves, that the narrator of the novel, after long years of disappointed excursions in the world, counts as travel. Even our experience of books, he comes to believe, even of paintings, as the example of Swann makes plain, can end in sterility if they do not spark explorations of our own. And yet, for all that, I came to believe that the sharp surge of joy when I had first heard the word *Cambrai* pronounced aloud—so like the anticipatory joy that had flooded the narrator when a scent or sound or taste signaled the presence of a past self trembling toward recovery—could only mean that the narrator's world had entered the sphere of my own past, that his memories had become my own, and that the world of the book must certainly draw me back, at last, into the distant reaches of myself.

And so it was, finally, as a beneficent spirit presiding like a watchful patron saint over my stay in his native land that Proust's narrator assumed a presence in Avesnes. I scarcely gave him a thought—but that was because there was no need to. His was the voice, once heard, that continued to murmur whether I was listening or not. But if the world went quiet for a moment, there it was, with its astonishing convictions. However terrible our discouragements and griefs, however lengthy our journey toward understanding, the selves we had considered lost forever or, worse, have never even missed, may be restored if we are patiently attentive to our own inner promptings. His was the voice of possibility, of hope.

Diary of a Country Priest

———

La lecture est au seuil de la vie spirituelle; elle peut nous y introduire; elle ne la constitue pas.

Reading is at the threshold of the spiritual life; it can introduce us to it; it does not constitute it.

—*Sur la lecture*, Marcel Proust

I

One drizzly Saturday afternoon in early December when the white fog at the windows was already being swallowed by darkness at three o'clock in the afternoon, when the cold moist air of Avesnes had begun to settle in our bones, the comforting notion of a leek and potato soup thickened with *crème fraîche* carried me up the steps and into the little storeroom where I remembered having seen a copper pot. In the half-light, I stumbled over a pile of books I'd examined on my first visit to this room and had dismissed as without interest at a moment when my thoughts were all with Emma. They had seemed to be devotional books from the turn of the century, of a piece with the baroque bust of Christ that long ago we'd removed from the mantel and hidden away here among the old mirrors and fans. There had been one, I remembered, *Journal d'un curé de campagne* by Georges Bernanos, that had made me think of Emma's desperate attempt to speak to the priest at Yonville, had brought sharply to mind his soup-stained cassock and terrifying banalities. But on this December afternoon, perhaps because I had been thinking of starting a journal—had remembered my promise to myself made on the balcony of our lost home at Igbobi, the trumpet flowers gleaming in the dusk, the shuffle of C.'s sandals on the stairs; or perhaps had remembered a girl named Catherine Earnshaw who in distress had dipped her pen in ink one cold rainy Sunday on the edge of the moors and written her story in the margin of a book—the title of this unknown book caused me to pick it up and put it in the bottom of the pot.

The whisper on the first page of *Journal d'un curé de campagne* of someone talking to himself from the depths of his own loneliness: "When I first sat down before this child's copy-book I tried to concentrate, to withdraw into myself as though I were examining my conscience before confession. And yet my real conscience was not revealed by that inner light—usually so dispassionate and penetrating, passing over details, showing up the whole. It seemed to skim the surface of another consciousness, previously unknown to me, a cloudy mirror in which I feared that a face might suddenly appear. Whose face? Mine, perhaps. A forgotten, rediscovered face. . . .

"When writing of oneself one should show no mercy. Yet why at the first attempt to discover one's own truth does all inner strength seem to melt away in floods of self-pity and tenderness and rising tears. . . ."

Were these the words that leapt from the first pages of the book that night when—following our dinner of soup and endives and Camembert, after the babies were asleep—I sat down by the stove with a piece of dark chocolate to begin reading? Or were the words those of the opening: "My parish is bored stiff; no other word for it. Like so many others! We can see them being eaten up by boredom, and we can't do anything about it. Some day perhaps we shall catch it ourselves—become aware of the cancerous growth within us. You can keep going a long time with that in you."

It may have been either, or both, but beginning to read the book is confused in memory with a tap on the door, Mme Druet come to tell us that a man, a miner who worked in the quarry down the road, had died an hour earlier almost within view of the house on the route de Landrecies. She stood in the doorway in her blue smock, hands raised in commiseration and alarm, cheeks mottled with the cold. A neighbor had stopped just now to tell them. He worked in the quarry, this man, and had been walking back to Saint-Hilaire, where he lived. He hadn't been hit by a car, that was the wonder of it. There wasn't a mark on him. A *crise de coeur*? The headlights of a car had discovered him, lying by the side of the road in the rain.

She had gone sadly away, shaking her head, but when I sat down again to resume reading, although the words seemed to stick flat against the page, floating beneath was a figure lying on its back, each part of him—fingers, stubbled chin, thighs, penis, knees—soaking up the rain. And then gradually, as I read on, other figures joined him, heads lolling, faces slippery with mud and blood, bodies flung across a field like the ones stretching away from the route de Landrecies, or sitting bolt upright in a trench, headless. The names of towns mentioned in the book—Lille, Arras, Amiens—were the ones we heard every day in the streets of Avesnes, towns we'd visited ourselves. I looked in the front of the book to see when it was first published: 1936. Three years before the outbreak of the Second World War: and within its pages scarcely any mention of the war on whose savaged ground we walked as did the young man keeping the journal, who seemed to be about the same age as ourselves.

And yet here, apparently, was the story of someone who was dying and who both knew it and did not. The voice seemed to be saying all it knew, confessing, in the manner of a journal, what could be said nowhere else: all the humiliations and embarrassments and disappointments, the passing moments of hope, that made up the round of his days, confessions that recalled me to my own disappointments, my own baffled hopes. And yet this voice seemed to be speaking into a silence so profound that the only worthy response would have been that of death. Like Emma, like those lying broken on the battlefields of northern France, the priest was someone destined to die young.

That was it: he had only a brief moment in which to work out his destiny. And while I still believed I would live a long, long time, it was in Avesnes, walking at noon one day into the foyer we shared with the Druets and turning to hang up my coat on a standing rack that had a mirror poised above it, that I caught sight of a line etched beneath my eye. The first, I thought. Here it begins. In Avesnes.

I'd woken that night with a pounding heart. I'd nursed the baby, felt the bones in her lovely head, kissed the nape of her neck, her apricot cheeks, but when she was in her cot again, I'd fallen back on the pillow staring into the dark. C. was asleep beside me. What now? Our lives were slipping away in this blood-soaked country where the earth was crowded with skeletons of the young. In this bed, where the German general had slept, our lovemaking went on unabated. What could this mean? There was something I couldn't see, couldn't make sense of. It wasn't about C. and myself, our story together. It was about my own life, separate, still waiting in the shadows, unexplored.

The mirror told me the tape was running out, how quickly I didn't know, and for the first time the specter of my own end rose to meet me. My life in hiding, I thought, was my life in death, seen in dark relief, as against a backdrop. If time allowed, my face would fall into ruin. My greatest certainty was that I would die. My greatest uncertainty, when.

Up until now I'd spent the time in Avesnes in a state of barely disguised regret. *This* was not my life, not this little town with its war memorial and courthouse and *mairie* flying its sad tricolor, its houses of gray stone and bricks waiting mutely beneath a somber sky. It was a parenthesis, an aberration. I'd struck an awkward peace with these buildings clustered around a church on the edge of the lowlands, had in some complicated way come to resign myself to the idea that my life here had been suspended. It would resume after we'd left Avesnes behind. Following the long day alone with the babies, I'd tried to take myself in hand, was determined to banish the ghost of Emma, not to complain. I was loftily prepared to make the most of it. No, I wouldn't concede defeat. But I still felt my life was on hold.

But if my life was on hold, where was I and what was I doing? It seemed there was no room to ask. Never had I lived as I was living now. Every minute was used up in caring for the babies, in preparing classes or teaching them, in keeping us all in clean clothes and fed, keeping us warm. All of which work C. wholeheartedly shared. At last in bed at night, I struggled to stay awake, to read a page or two of a novel— the morning would come in a flash, the daily round begin all over again—but the book fell from my hands, sleep swiftly advancing like a tide. I was almost never alone. Sometimes, desperate, I snatched up the scuttle and ran out to the coal bin in back, pausing a moment between shovelfuls to gaze out on pastures sunk in early morning mist or mute beneath the afternoon rain. Breathing in the air, I thought of nothing. I was alive, that was all.

The other moment I could be alone, or at least silent, was on

Sunday mornings when I went to Mass at Saint-Nicolas, leaving
the babies behind with C. Here I hoped to find something of
what I had sought in novels, a story, a world that opened out
beyond my own inner walls, a place for contemplation, eternity
in an hour. Had it been the same for my great-grandmother
who'd come from Ireland with all her children during the
Famine? Who, after her husband's death that followed quickly
on her own arrival, had by herself worked a little farm in the
Mohawk Valley? She'd owned a few cows, and it occurred to
me that her life in many ways must have resembled M and
Mme Druet's: there would have been no time for reading a
novel, certainly, which I now understood to be the privilege
of the wealthy, the leisured. No, her prayer book, the gospels,
would have been her only reading. Inside her church—perhaps
called St. Brigid's, where a Celtic cross had been carved into the
altar and the mass said in Irish—she may have savored a brief
moment of reflection, have tried to make sense of where she'd
come from and where she was going.

And yet, on entering Saint-Nicolas I realized I'd been hoping
for something that would not be delivered for the asking.
Even in these September days, the chill was penetrating and a
stale odor of incense and dank mustiness seeped from its stone
walls. This church seemed strikingly foreign. I was familiar
with St. Dominic's, in Yaba, where people sat on benches in
long rows; and the church I'd known from childhood had
pews. But here there were chairs with cane seats that could be
moved around as you liked, little leather kneelers folding down
in back. Nor had I ever been in a church with so many side
altars, so many painted wooden saints perched on pedestals,
looking down from walls and columns. In one side chapel the
space above the altar was entirely filled by a large painting
depicting a seated St. Anne teaching her little daughter Mary
to read, bending down to her with a scroll. In another chapel,

another painting, this time of Mary greeting Elizabeth, two pregnant women embracing. Looking more closely at the golden plaques beneath, I saw these were the work of Louis Watteau of Lille. Episodes in Mary's life were familiar subjects, but I didn't know much about the painted French saints, who they were or when they'd lived: Saint Louis in a high golden crown, gathering up with one hand a sky-blue mantel adorned with gilded fleur-de-lys; Sainte Germaine wearing a peasant's blouse, roses caught in her red apron, a lamb at her feet. And then, of course, Jeanne d'Arc, another girl of the countryside, *La Pucelle*, as she called herself, but portrayed here in a cuirass, clutching a sword.

There was also a stone tomb containing the bones of a husband and wife who must have been familiar with the story of Jeanne d'Arc, a legend in her own time: a couple who were themselves breathing still when she was burned at the stake in 1431. Atop the tomb, effigies presented them side by side—he dead in 1433, she in 1467—both with hands pressed piously together at their breasts: a full-length Olivier de Blois in complicated armor, his genitals protected by a separate shield that cast its own faint shadow, a gauntlet at his feet; his wife, another Jeanne, in a gown that lapped at her toes, a gown any French woman might have worn in any era. When Olivier was interred here, the church of Saint-Nicolas was already old, two hundred years or more, and it may have been that the widowed Jeanne herself was present, standing beside the stone—precisely where I was standing now—into which the date of her own death would be chiseled thirty-four years later. There they were, this couple, lying side by side, just as C. and I lay every night in our bed. But Olivier and Jean were dust and we were not.

I looked around at the parishioners as they assembled, and although most were the people we passed every day in the town and knew nothing about, I did recognize some of them: there up near the front was one of my students, Chantal, and her father, who was the butcher on the *place* and with his cleaver struck off a chop. In his *boucherie* a recording announced: *"La Maison, vous presente . . . ,"* words I sometimes repeated as I placed on the table a slice of pâté, a bit of sausage. I saw other students as well, recognized the boy who earlier that morning had jumped from the van in front of our house with the baguettes for Mme Druet. And an old woman bent double I'd seen more than once in the *place* tapping her way with a stick. There was a couple, too, directly in front of me, he with dark hair, she with light, and two children a little older than ours. I'd seen them before, I thought, but couldn't remember from where.

I found I could follow the Mass because I knew the prayers already, most of them. When the gospel was read I recognized the words *Lazarus* and *homme riche* and knew it was the story of the rich man dressed in purple and fine linens and the beggar Lazarus, who lay outside the rich man's gate, starving for the crumbs that fell from his table, so wretched the dogs came and licked his sores. But when Lazarus died, the story goes, the angels carried him straight to Abraham's breast. The rich man, on the other hand, found himself in fiery torment. He called out to Father Abraham, begging that Lazarus dip his finger in cool water and drop it on his burning tongue. Only a drop! But no, Abraham answered, the chasm was now too great between the two, there was no passing between. During his life the rich man had been well satisfied but now it was Lazarus who was finding consolation for his many sufferings.

Maybe because I was hearing the story in a language not my own, I seemed to be hearing it for the first time. Then the priest was speaking. Was he saying, as I thought he was, that it was the rich man who needed the poor man all along? That though it was true the poor needed bread, the rich were more needy than the poor? I looked to see if I could learn anything from the faces around me. But I couldn't read them, they reflected nothing back to me. And so it was that week after week we would gather to listen to another story: the prodigal son, the Good Samaritan, the woman taken in adultery. You could say we were sharing something intimate, these stories of tender compassion and hope. But then, I wondered, why did we all seem so detached from each other? What was it we felt?

Until I picked up Bernanos's novel that Saturday evening in December I had no name for it. But with the first sentences everything became clear: "My parish is bored stiff. No other word for it." Boredom, that was the word, exactly. Boredom, it occurred to me, is suffering taken for granted: a disguise for hopelessness. And I wondered if that was the expression they saw on my own face, a nagging discontent that never quite broke through into sorrow.

II

From the first moment, when Mme Druet had tapped on the door and admitted Avesnes into the room where a new voice was breaking the silence, this town of which I knew so little instructed my reading of *Diary of a Country Priest*. This was not a question of an already familiar presence— Emma or the narrator of Proust's novel—coming forward out of the mist to shimmer for a moment before beating a graceful retreat because the place, the moment, didn't extend a welcome. In the case of this new book it was the region itself, all the suffering that lay both above and below its soil, the griefs of the ages, that invited and opened the way for an emerging shape. Avesnes seemed to peer through the print on the page, as if its hidden face were that of the priest bent over the copybook in which he was writing, as if it were impossible to perceive one without the other.

The old world: that was where we were, the reason we'd come. As far back as the seventh century, an abbey had existed at Le Maroilles whose records made explicit a period of three months—from the feast of St. John on June 24 until the first of October, feast of Saint Remy—as the time required to turn milk into the wheels of cheese we bought in the Place du General Leclerc on Friday mornings. And as for M Druet herding the cows from the pastures on the first day of November to the warmth of the barn: that didn't have to do at all with the feast of All Saints, as I'd imagined, but with a custom that predated the arrival of Christianity. It wasn't, of course, that people had suffered any longer on this ground than any other: it was just that it was possible to look into faces—whether in the classroom, or the *boulangerie*, or in the Druets' kitchen—and know that beneath this same sky, surrounded by these same fields, sheltered by these same stones, faces resembling these in cut and expression had for long centuries been young and grown old.

To be young here was to be everywhere surrounded by evidence of the not-so-young-anymore, of the long dead. This I knew. As for the young country priest—the "I" bearing no other name—who both knows he's harboring a fatal illness and does not, his journal reflects the urgent need to weigh despair against hope, doubt against faith, to see and feel and act while there is still time.

A child of the poor, he is in hidden sympathy with those who are, in whatever way, on the outside looking in, those who have inherited the bitter isolation of want from their earliest days. While he was still a child, his aunt took him in. "She kept a little pub just outside Lens, a horrible wooden shanty where they sold gin to miners who were too poor to go anywhere else. The nearest school was a couple of miles away, and I used to do my homework squatting behind the bar on the floor—that is to say a few rotting boards. The dank reek of earth came up between them, earth which was always wet, the reek of mud. On pay-nights our customers didn't even go outside to relieve themselves; they would pass water where they stood, and I was so terrified, crouching behind the bar, that in the end I'd fall asleep. But the teacher was kind to me, lending me books. It was there I read the childhood memories of Maxim Gorki."

And then: "The first realization of misery is fierce indeed. Blessed be he who has saved a child's heart from despair! It is a thing most people know so little about, or forget because it would frighten them too much. Amongst the poor as amongst the rich, a little boy is all alone, as lonely as a king's son. At all events in our part of the world, distress is not shared, each creature is alone in his distress; it belongs only to him, like his face and his hands."

But who were the poor in Avesnes and where did they live? They seemed to be nowhere in sight. As far as I could see, there were the well-to-do landowners like Soeur Marie Joliette's father, and then, like M and Mme Druet, the ones hired to live on his land and care for it. There were those, too, who lived in the large brick houses in town whose lighted windows we passed in winter returning from the Institut, where through lace curtains we could catch a glimpse of chairs covered in red velvet like the ones in the unused salon upstairs. We thought that the people who lived in these large houses in town must be those we'd heard called *la bourgeoisie*. Some, we knew, had property elsewhere; one kept an apartment on the Côte d'Azur. Of course, too, there were laborers working in the street, servants, miners who worked in the quarry. But where they lived we didn't know, nor whether they might be called "the poor." We had seen men, too, with an arm or a leg missing, blind men with badly scarred faces, but these we knew had been in a war: quite another thing. I thought of the miners Van Gogh had painted in a region of Belgium that was only a stone's throw across the border from Avesnes and wondered if in fact I'd seen poverty and failed to recognize it.

Then one evening, perhaps a month after the drizzly night when the man had died on the route de Landrecies, I absent-mindedly turned left instead of right leaving the Institut Ste-Thérèse after a *reunion* and found myself walking in the dark down a steep narrow passage that descended in a series of broad stone slabs arranged at intervals to make steps. This was the passage we had been told about but had never seen that connected the upper town with its *place* and shops and schools to the lower town where Vauban's fortifications stood their ground. Again it was raining, with a chill in the air that settled in the marrow of the bones, and I wondered if I should turn back or see where the steps would lead. It was only gradually that I became aware of dwellings opening onto the steps, some with doors ajar. In one I saw the bright glow of a lantern on a dirt floor and then by its light, scampering up the steps, a child wearing a man's jacket, his feet wrapped in rags. His blue eyes met mine for only an instant as he ran past me on the glistening stone.

I immediately turned around where I was and went back

up the steps again until I was in the *place*. I was in a mild panic. I felt as if I'd violated someone's secret, had stepped uninvited into a space where I had no business. But no, even as I found my way past the *boulangerie* where flayed rabbits hung in the lighted window, past the elegant *mairie*, shivering myself now, I knew that wasn't it at all. It was shock I felt and like Avesnes I'd resolutely turned my back on the boy with the blazing eyes just as the rich man had on Lazarus. Avesnes preferred not to see him at all. And neither did I. I already knew of secrets one kept from oneself. But now that I had seen the boy I knew it was impossible to return to innocence.

In the following days, the child seemed to appear everywhere. I couldn't turn a corner, enter a classroom, without catching a glimpse of a small figure that disappeared as soon as I looked again. He was the vanishing guarantor, the signature attached to the words I was reading. Because here, running in and out of the pages of the book, was an oblique record of the ongoing struggle not to lose all hope in a world where injustice is the order of the day and the poor accused of their sufferings. Where God, even to the priest desperately trying to pray, remains silent. And where the struggle, as often as not, takes the form of modern self-doubt and fear—dread of one's own incapacities; the wincing away from what one knows is ridiculous in oneself, absurd; the constant sense that one has mismanaged things. "Fool that I am! I know nothing of my people. I never shall! I can't profit by my mistakes: they upset me too much. I must be one of those weak, miserable creatures, always so full of the best intentions, whose whole lives oscillate between ignorance and despair."

❧

If I'd complained of the cold, of the struggle to survive loneliness in this place, the riveting exchange of glances with the boy on the steps now stopped my tongue. I read the book slowly, a few pages a day throughout the winter months and on into the spring. This was only in part because my French still didn't allow for more, especially at night when I had trouble keeping my eyes open and wanted nothing more than to collapse into English. It was also because, however long I lived in Avesnes, I wanted to live within the covers of this book. It was in its pages alone there seemed space enough for a burgeoning sorrow. We had recently heard about the outbreak of the war in Biafra, in the Igboland that Achebe had described in *Things Fall Apart*. In my imagination the shattered bodies flung over the tops of trenches had been joined by others. We were, of course, writing letters back and forth to Ben, who had been our most constant Igbo companion. But it was unbearable to think that bodies of the schoolboys we'd taught—schoolboys so beloved we had scarcely any room within us for the French girls who sat before us—were even now soaking the rain forests of eastern Nigeria with their blood.

We were ignorant of the poor of Avesnes, but what did we know of anyone else? What about the butchers and bakers and the stationmaster? The doctors and lawyers? Their children were our students, the ones we met every day in the classroom. From the first I'd recognized uneasily that my tentative approach to the girls was lacking the quick warmth that had come so easily at Igbobi. Their names—Marie-Claude or Marie-Pierre or Marie-Françoise—were more difficult for me to remember than Yoruba and Igbo and

Hausa names. The girls wore uniforms, white blouses and navy blue skirts, navy knee socks, just as the boys at Igbobi had worn khaki. But these were schoolgirls, not boys, and my own adolescence was still too recent, too threatening, to regard any version of it at all without dismay.

Just a few years ago, a schoolgirl myself, I'd read out of desperation, read straight through entire days, weekends, holidays. Was this a novel in which I would recognize myself, I asked of each one? Would it help me survive, tell me how to live? I read *Jane Eyre* breathlessly; here was an outsider who after many struggles would be chosen, adored, in compensation for her lonely days. And yet, perhaps because I'd read *Wuthering Heights* earlier, the story of *Jane Eyre* seemed to me not quite trustworthy. It was seductive, but I feared took me further away from what I was looking for. I was wary of stories that ended too well, that ended—after whatever soul-changing conflicts—in perfect contentment. They seemed to me some version of the "happily ever after" story that Miss Hughes had taught us to mistrust. Art would be our consolation, our hope, but life would continue to exact a stern price.

I knew there were girls like myself among our students, isolated, living in books, but I wasn't sure how to recognize them. Besides, I felt a growing despair about my teaching. What was it that was lacking in myself that had been abundantly present at Igbobi, however inept and awkward I'd been? In class we spoke a stilted, earnest English that never quite broke through into self-revelation. I blamed my lack of connection with my students on language, not wanting to name the more important thing in myself that was missing. The novels some of the girls read and reread, the poetry, were written in a language that I was only now learning. Outside of class, one or another of my students sometimes seemed to search me out. She'd start by speaking in cautious English, but the moment passion carried her into rapid French was the moment I was no longer certain I understood. She might have been saying one thing, but I was afraid to respond for fear she'd said the exact opposite, that I hadn't picked up a hidden, swallowed negative that changed the meaning of everything.

Sometimes we had *reunions* with the other teachers when one by one each girl was discussed. *"Bonne famille"* was sometimes pronounced approvingly of one of them, designating some social standing we didn't know how to gauge. But we did know these were the people who invited us for a midday dinner Sunday after Sunday, the parents of our students, people who gave us their attention while we spoke haltingly of our trip to visit the cathedral at Amiens, whom we tried to turn into teachers of French, stopping them in the middle of a sentence to ask the meaning of a word. They were endlessly kind, seemed never to give up on us. C. one day tried out the expression he'd learned from one of his vocabulary books, "un brin de causette," thinking it was slang for "a chat." Our student's father for a moment looked blank, then hesitantly, with great courtesy, explained that particular expression had probably not been used since the eighteenth century. Afterward, between ourselves, we employed it tirelessly, working it into every possible context.

The student of the family we were visiting would very often help amuse the babies during the long meal, play with them, sometimes afterward show us her own room, where a poster might be pinned to the wall of Françoise Hardy, her long dark hair and bangs, her lonely eyes. We'd heard Hardy on the radio, knew the song that was everywhere, *Tous les garçons et les filles*, a song about love hunger, about wandering alone while everyone else of the same age walks the streets two by two, holding hands, looking into each other's eyes, happily falling in love without any fear of tomorrow. A song I intimately understood from my own days as a teenager.

We were grateful for people's efforts to relieve our isolation and vowed to each other we would never forget the untiring welcome given to us in France. When we'd thank our hosts as we finally said goodbye, they'd answer that it was all *tout à fait normal*, the most ordinary thing in the world, but to us it seemed as if they'd gone to an extraordinary amount of trouble. It also seemed they knew more about us than we did about them, forgetting that in fact we said very little about our own lives and that in their eyes it was we who were the foreigners, only briefly passing through.

Then one evening the older sister of one of our students, whose family had invited us several times, stopped by in her car to meet us; she'd been studying in New York, was just back in Avesnes and wanted to speak English. As the night wore on and we opened a second bottle of wine, she told us about her father, how one day she'd encountered him on a street in Lille with a woman who was certainly younger than herself, how it had always been like this, by now she had nothing for him but contempt. That her mother was beyond noticing, was too proud to speak of it, but that she herself felt betrayed—did he have no respect for her either, they'd been close when she was a little girl—and since her return to Avesnes was struggling with a spirit of profound hopelessness. We had listened, wondering if we should stop her, but too breathlessly intrigued by news of lives we knew so little about to interrupt or change the subject. After that night, the Sunday meals took on a different character. Somewhere beneath the fitful conversations that carried us from *crudités* to *potage* to *rôti* to *salade* to *Maroilles* to *dessert*, the voice of the journal spoke more insistently. Who was I to dismiss the struggle with boredom and despair, the hidden sorrows, of those at whose tables we were sitting? And what did it mean that I continued to hold myself aloof from these lives? Was it pride of a kind I couldn't recognize?

It wasn't until early April that I reached the great scene that stands at the center of the *Diary of a Country Priest*, the moment when the priest visits the château in order to speak to the countess of his fear that her daughter is in danger of killing herself. It was impossible to picture a château—not something like Blois or Amboise or Chenonceaux—but a château of the kind where this encounter might have taken place, a little château that might have housed a foolish father, a daughter outraged by his casual infidelities not so much to her mother as to herself: in fact, a *ménage* startlingly like the one described to us by our visitor. Picturing the château wouldn't have mattered so much, except that having stumbled on the child running up the steps it seemed important to have some idea of the place to which the priest eventually came.

And then one April evening, exulting in the lengthening days, we found ourselves driving at twilight along country roads that were new to us. On either side stretched pastures of deepening green, broken only by the old gray stone of farmhouses and barns. We were commenting on how much of the countryside we had still to explore when suddenly, in the glimmering light, it was there, unmistakably: a stately house set back from the road, a pair of high steps leading up with a flourish to the door, long windows upstairs and down. Narrow brick chimneys rose from the slated roof and beneath, from the mansard, looked out those strange round eyes found in houses of substance, *les yeux du boeuf.* There was no one inside, everything was closed tight, so we got out of the car and looked through a pair of wrought-iron gates that had crests worked into their tracery. In the bright new grass we could see yellow jonquils, an abundance of them, gleaming in the dusk. It was these jonquils that gave the château its air of melancholy, of having been abandoned. The long windows were dark and shadowless, the jonquils blooming for the open sky.

So it was here, then, it might have taken place, the encounter I had been trying to imagine, again the struggle with despair, not on a battlefield, but in a place like this one. Here the proud countess might have countered the priest's concern by saying her daughter was horribly afraid of death, afraid of a sore throat, afraid of everything, and here he might have answered that those are the very ones who kill themselves; those who don't dare look into the void throw themselves in for fear of falling. And here she might have asked if he himself was one of those, like her daughter, afraid to die, and heard him answer that he was; heard him say later on that hell was nothing else but that state where we are no longer able to love, no longer able to recognize those dearest to us. And here later on that night, the transformed countess—a rich woman given hope by a poor priest, I thought, remembering the homily about the rich man and Lazarus, the beggar—might have died very suddenly, at peace.

As the days grew longer and the cows were brought back out of the barns and into the pastures where, after milking, they passed the short hours of darkness, I read more and more slowly, sometimes rereading lines from earlier sections. The strawberries ripened, the flies returned. A paragraph a day, approaching the end, and then a few sentences: "Oh miracle— thus to be able to give what we ourselves do not possess, sweet miracle of our empty hands! Hope which was shriveling in my heart flowered again in hers; the spirit of prayer which I thought lost in me forever was given back to her."

It would have been impossible to have spent a night in the bed where the German general had slept without knowing that in the morning the book would be waiting. The book took account of the world's injustice, its inclination toward unspeakable depravity. But each sentence of the priest's diary was filled with the clear light of an intelligence informed by love. In a few short weeks we would be leaving Avesnes. Paris beckoned as seductively as ever, and afterwards we'd go on to Provence, but now my delight in our departure seemed suspect: why should I be so glad to leave a place where I'd spent a year? There would be no wrenching goodbyes.

The priest's diary had struck into visibility the burning lives of those around me, but it seemed I'd missed something essential, I wasn't sure what. The book had provided a diagram of a place, a guide to the region, the town. Here you will find the poor, here the little château where the Countess surrendered her pride at last and was released to joy. But nowhere in the town had I recognized the young priest's face, the living face of compassion. I must have encountered it, but unknowingly. It came to me that throughout our time in Avesnes I'd looked at the town and its people, the people gathered for mass at Saint-Nicolas, through the lens of fear. And nowhere had this reserve been more striking than with my students. There had been a failure of imagination, of love. The unlived life looked out at me from the here and now. It was the life I'd turned away from. I thought of the shivering boy on the wet steps and it occurred to me that my reluctance to see what was there constituted an act of despair all its own. So it had been with that other boy, Norman de Carteret. So it had been in Badagry. I had only to think of the country priest. He'd hated to die but had spent himself lavishly, had spent everything he had. In losing his life he'd found it. In holding onto my own, I'd forfeited what might have been. To live, I considered, was to choose what was given. Now the time was gone.

During the final days, crating our belongings so that we could travel lightly to the south, waving away the flies that had returned with the first heat, I followed the approach of the summer solstice as the keeper of the journal followed his own slow course toward the end. In the shadow of a dripping hedge, the cows lowing just beyond, he passes out, is discovered by a child who brings water and washes his face. He makes a friend, realizing "that friendship can break out between two people, with that sudden violence which generally is only attributed to the revelation of love." His new friend Olivier takes him for a ride on the back of his silver motorcycle and he very briefly tastes the heady joys of youth, riding at full speed, hair streaming, over roads he's walked step by weary step, a taste only long enough to acquaint him with all he's leaving behind.

He visits a doctor in Lille, a doctor who is his double, suffering with the help of morphine from a fatal illness

like his own. It is there in Lille—facing the death that will
overtake him the next morning on a camp bed in his friend's
apartment—that he writes that human agony is, above all,
an act of love. I wasn't sure I understood but felt this was a
profound intuition I might grasp in time.

On the final Saturday we were to spend in Avesnes, we visited
the market, knowing this would be the last time. Our classes
now concluded, we'd decided to take a break from packing
by going to town to buy a baguette, some strawberries, a last
Maroilles. We were standing on the old stones of the *place*,
watching the farmer from whom we always bought cheese
wrap our purchase in a page from *La Voix du Nord*, when
the carillon in the steeple of Saint-Nicolas, high above our
heads, suddenly threw off a shower of chimes. Once again
it wheezed, as if taking breath, before solemnly delivering
twelve bongs, one after another, at intervals that allowed
the reverberations to ripple out in the mild clear air. On the
final stroke a young woman with straight blond hair falling
to her shoulders appeared with a little girl at her side and
introduced herself. She was Geneviève Delavoy and had
seen us in town, had been told we were in Avesnes for a year.
And this was Anne, she said, looking down at her child: she
had a birthday next week, would be six years old. Anne held
up one hand, fingers wide apart, and the index finger of the
other. The next moment Geneviève's husband had joined us
and introduced himself as Pierre. With him was a boy who
looked about three or four. He had dark hair, like Pierre,
the same dark eyes, and yet the slightly bedazzled look of
Geneviève.

We explained we were just about to leave Avesnes, that

we were even now saying goodbye to the market. Are you free later on, Geneviève asked. Why didn't we come by about six. We'd feed the children first so they could play while we seized the chance for at least one visit. And where did they live? In the rue d'Aulnoy, down behind the hospital, we'd easily find it, a brick house with a flight of stairs in front. And so it was we heard the bells of Saint-Nicolas strike eight that night from somewhere far above as we sat round a table in the *ville-bas*, eating ragout, sipping wine, eagerly talking with another young couple about our lives. In our desire to understand one another the barrier of language fell away: it seemed our French had become serviceable. They'd met as students in Paris—Pierre at Science Polytechnique, Geneviève at Université de Paris, Vincennes—and had come to live in Avesnes after they'd married. It was here that Pierre had grown up, in a house nearby where his parents still lived and his grandparents before them. Now he managed the family business in heavy farm machinery and dairy equipment. He looked at us from behind glittering lenses, his gaze intelligent, restless. And Geneviève? She was from Bretagne and taught French literature at the *lycée*. Her mother had died when she was a little girl, and in the summers they visited her father—had we seen much of France?—in the village she'd known as a child, fields of grass threaded with daisies running down to the sea. The children loved it. And ourselves? Who were we? Where did we come from? We told them about Africa, how we happened to be in Avesnes. They listened with keen interest, wanted to know about Nigeria, about the places where we'd been born. And what about our year in Avesnes? Had we been all right here?

A knock at the door and Pierre brought in an old man

wearing a beret and a coat with holes at the elbows. His shoes were tied together with string. Geneviève pulled out a chair at the table, set before him a bowl of soup, half a baguette. Pierre poured a glass of wine. The old man raised his glass very slightly to the company, made a little flourish in the air, before taking a first sip. He said nothing and, when finished eating, stood up, bowed to Geneviève, and went his way. When he was gone I asked, hesitantly, if he came often. "Ça arrive," Genevieve answered matter-of-factly, shrugging her shoulder, smiling at me a little. And with a blaze of recognition I knew I was looking into the face of compassion that had eluded me until now.

We found it hard to take our leave, but when we at last gathered up the babies, Geneviève and Pierre said what a pity, to have met like this at the last minute, just as we were leaving Avesnes. They'd have been glad to have kept the children while we'd had a weekend alone in Paris. But now we were already friends. Who knew what life would bring? They stood together at the doorway as we went down the front brick steps in a state resembling jubilation.

A full moon was rising above the town. As we drove home through the streets in a state of hushed and grateful silence, then out onto the route de Landrecies, a milky light flooded the road and pastures, bringing into vivid relief the shadow of a barn, a solitary tree, a telephone pole: things were at last declaring themselves, the unseen giving itself away. Three cows, heads together, stood in silent conference. The sheen on white daisies and buttercups shimmered across the fields, like silk. On this one evening what I hadn't thought to ask for had risen to meet me. I'd received just enough taste of it to know what I'd missed.

⁂

A few days later, on the evening before we were to leave Avesnes, everything at last packed and ready for departure, we stood outside the house with M and Mme Druet watching Patrick drive the milked cows back across the route de Landrecies and into the pastures. It would be the shortest night of the year. With the moment so quickly approaching when we would no longer see each other, when on either side our lives would once again sink into the mysterious unknown, an uneasy shyness seemed to overtake us all. When Patrick joined us at last he stood with his arms loose at his sides, not saying a word. And although Mme Druet did her best—now we had two little walking children, how quickly they'd grown!—we finally took leave of each other with an obscure sense of shame, as if perhaps we had never known each other in the least, had allowed what was most important of all to go unsaid.

We went inside, telling each other that tomorrow we'd say goodbye. The windows were open to let in the night, and there was still just enough daylight to allow a glimpse from the room upstairs of the steeple at Saint-Hilaire—the name, I suddenly remembered, of the church in Combray, the steeple that the narrator's grandmother had said if it could play the piano she was sure would really *play.* I had reserved the next-to-last page of the journal for tonight and then had planned for the morning the last of all, an italicized page, written in the form, I could see, of a letter. But I felt too much unquiet, at first, to read. I could think only of the anxiety and boredom in which my days had been spent, the hours by the smoking stove struggling to keep the babies warm, the fog at the windows, the slow drizzle that had fallen on the trenches. Why could I not, at the very least, have responded with some show of gratitude to Patrick's invitation to come watch them kill the pig? His shy offer had been inspired by motives I had not even tried to imagine. Now, at the point of departure, I could at last forgive Emma her vanities, but could less easily forgive my own. There had been many, like Patrick, who'd recognized our loneliness and tried to console the outsider, Lazarus at the gate. And yet I hadn't been able to see myself, as they had, as one of the poor, in need of a crumb. So it was that, sitting at the window, I finally picked up the book and read the last words of the journal: "How easy it is to hate oneself! True grace is to forget. Yet if pride could die in us, the supreme grace would be to love oneself in all simplicity—as one would love any one of those who themselves have suffered and loved in Christ."

The sky, tomorrow night, would be the same sky, spreading over Avesnes and Paris alike. But by then Avesnes for us would already have become a place containing a completed year of our past. Paris was all ahead, but for Avesnes it was now too late. I thought how, no matter in what simplicity I might try to accept my failures of generosity both towards myself and the people of Avesnes, I would always regret that here on this spot of earth I'd kept myself apart.

And so, not waiting for morning, I read the friend in Lille's account of the priest's death, of his last words: "But what does it matter? Grace is everywhere."

À la recherche du temps perdu

I

We read in the front room of the ground-floor apartment, looking out on Claremont Avenue. The chairs were wide and deep, lamps ready on the table next to the sofa where Diana Trilling sat in her accustomed place and beside the chair where I had finally come to settle across the room. A double row of etchings hung in their frames above the sofa, and sometimes, when Diana was out of the room for a moment, I would set one straight that had been knocked askew. In a little elevated bookcase set in one wall, leaning against each other, were books recognizable from Lionel's essays: Ernest Jones's biography of Freud, the letters of Oscar Wilde, William Wordsworth's collected poems. And lying broadside, a picture book on Marcel Proust that Lionel had given Diana one Valentine's Day.

It was in this room, for ten years, that I read aloud to Diana Trilling every week. Her eyesight, by 1987, had badly deteriorated and she had trouble making out the printed page. Some years we met on Mondays, others on Wednesdays or Thursdays. If something interfered so that one of us couldn't arrange to be free that day, we tried to find another time in the same week. We were dedicated to our readings, and although she might occasionally be ill, or I might be away for a month or more, we always resumed with a sense of relief. If there had been a long hiatus, or if one of us had something pressing to talk about, we might not read at all that day. But the book was always waiting, and when I arrived at her apartment at four in the afternoon, after the working day was over, we settled to the comfort of the unwinding story with a sense of arriving home.

A ginkgo tree stood on the sidewalk outside the window. In late May its leaves cast a green light in the room and, in the fall, as the afternoons grew short, the fan leaves flickered gold in the twilight. By November they would be lying at the base of the trunk like drifted snow and the branches in the window would be stark and bare. One afternoon in April 1996, six months before Diana died, I arrived to tell her that finally, after a long and punishing winter, a green mist was hanging in the trees on Riverside Drive and there, too, in the ginkgo just outside the window. "I don't believe a word of it," she cried. "It's an illusion of spring." Then, a moment later, "That would make a good title for a novel, wouldn't it?"

I had watched the tree grow from a sapling since the afternoon I first came to visit Diana in the fall of 1975, having met her by chance that summer in Venice. C. and I, with our three young children, had been spending the summer in the former Zaire on Lake Kivu, in Bukavu, working for the Peace Corps, and I had come ahead early to spend some days in Paris at the Bibliothèque Nationale. I was writing a dissertation on Proust and wanted to look at the manuscripts. But the city that the narrator of Proust's novel had visited with his mother was on my way and it would cost no more to stop there. It was Venice, the charmed city of his imagination, which he had seen resolve into a commonplace pile of stones when he was faced with the prospect of staying on alone after her departure. And it was Venice, I remembered, that Thomas Mann had chosen for his story of death and love.

One morning in late August, two days after my arrival, I found my way to the Scuola de San Giorgio degli Schiavoni, one of the city's confraternity houses, to look at the Carpaccios. The day was all white heat, but the interior of the Scuola was shadowy and cool. After a few minutes, when the dazzle of light had yielded to the startling particularity of the large canvases that lined the walls, I became aware of a man and a woman looking at one of them. The woman was describing aloud the monks streaming away in fright from Saint Jerome's lion, robes flying, bold streaks of black on white. She pointed out the book dropped in a tuft of grass, its center pages standing upright from its spine, the slippered foot of the frightened reader pushing off for greater speed. The man was silent, his head inclined toward hers. I knew they were the Trillings because my father, like Lionel and Langston Hughes and Lou Gehrig, had been a member of Columbia's class of 1925, and when I was a child I had sometimes accompanied him to Dean's Day to hear Lionel lecture. But I don't think I had ever seen Diana. I had spoken to no one since arriving in Venice, and so decided to leave the chapel at the same moment they did. On the steps, standing in the glare of noon, I asked if they were the Trillings. They looked at me in astonishment. We spoke for a few moments about the Carpaccios, and when there seemed little else to say, they asked would I like to join them for lunch.

We had ham sandwiches and frosty glasses of beer at a table under an awning. They told me they had been at Oxford for the past year and were on their way back to New York. I told

them I lived on Morningside Drive, also in the neighborhood
of Columbia, where my husband taught an African language:
Hausa. Yes, it was spoken in northern Nigeria and in Niger,
as well as throughout West Africa as a trading language. A
little like Swahili in East Africa. Then we spoke of Gabriel
García Márquez, of the new wave of South American writers,
and later the Ca' Rozzonico we had all happened on, where
Robert Browning and Elizabeth Barrett Browning had lived.
Diana said she was looking for the Danieli Hotel because
she had stayed there when she had come as a young woman
to Venice with her father. She couldn't remember where it
was but would like to find it. I told her I thought that when
Proust had visited Venice with his mother he, too, had stayed
at the Danieli. We spoke of whether we should order more
sandwiches. "But Li," Diana said, "you haven't eaten half
enough!" And when we were gathering our things to leave,
Diana, who had been concerned to hear I was traveling alone,
told me that I must certainly stop by their hotel when I felt
like it—wouldn't I do that?—and if I needed anything at all
I must not hesitate to ask.

I thanked them for the lunch and we parted. I already
knew that I would not stop by their hotel; it would be awkward
suddenly appearing and finding them resting or engaged with
other people. But I still had two more days in Venice and the
next morning turned a corner to find the Danieli Hotel with
its balconied windows looking out, past the Giudecca and San
Giorgio Maggiore, to the horizon where the low dunes of the
Lido floated in the hazy light. That afternoon I took the boat
out to the Lido and walked up and down trying to find the
spot where Aschenbach had grown sick with love. There was
the far reach of the sea, the beach with its bathing houses,
but I could find no hotel that fit the picture fixed in my
imagination. At last, climbing the steps of a shabby building

in need of paint, I glimpsed above its broad front entrance a faded sign stamped with the words I had been looking for: HOTELS DES BAINS.

On my last afternoon in Venice, sitting in the piazza on the steps of one of the three massive flagpoles that rise in front of San Marco, I spotted the Trillings sitting with friends at a table in front of one of the cafés. But some shyness, some fear of intruding, kept me from approaching. The pigeons were swirling overhead, the violins sobbing, the gold of San Marco was on fire, I had already visited the baptistery of the basilica where the sensation of uneven stones beneath his feet, revived years later, had given the narrator of Proust's novel his first intimations of the recovery of lost time. The sun was warm on the stones where I sat. I could see Diana and Lionel leaning back in their chairs facing the great sinking glitter of San Marco, could see the giants on the digital clock lifting their hammers to strike the hour. In one of those moments when anguish and joy seem indistinguishable—like those our music teacher, Miss Hughes, had long ago instructed us to watch for—I saw that here was a moment in time never to be recovered, that it was all sliding away as we sat in stillness, all vanishing with the shadow that imperceptibly, moment by moment, was quenching the facade of San Marco.

The next morning, on the way to the *vaporetto* that would take me to the station, I stopped in a coffee bar. I had passed enough days wandering the city alone and was not sorry to leave. Standing at the counter, I glimpsed Diana and Lionel sitting in the back against a wall. This was my farewell to Venice, and it might as well be my farewell to them. But why, I asked myself, hoisting my bag to my shoulder, is there always this reticence, this shrinking away, before drawing near another person? I greeted them and told Diana that I had found the Danieli. She had as well, yes, yes, it was right there, looking out over the sea, but of course it didn't look as she had remembered. I said I was just on my way to catch a train, was on my way out. "Call me," Diana said. "Call me, when we're all back in the city and we'll have tea."

And so our friendship began. Rushing along the street that September on my way to visit her for the first time, I thought to remember the number 35 Claremont by adding two to my age: thirty-three. I would leave her apartment knowing that Diana had turned sixty-eight that summer, was Jewish, and that she had a son named Jim who was in his mid-twenties; she would know that I was Catholic and had three young daughters. We would have agreed that parenthood bestowed a delight so intense that people without children must be protected from knowing what they were missing. And I would have privately decided, an opinion never to be reversed, that her outrageous sense of the ludicrous made her one of the funniest people I had ever met.

But what was remarkable about that first visit was the sense of wonder and relief I felt in being able to talk to an older woman not my mother about matters C. and I and all our friends endlessly discussed without much light. Because over the years our conversations had changed. In the fall of 1966 we'd returned after three years away to find ourselves strangers in a country we'd referred to as "home." At the University of Wisconsin in Madison where C. would study Hausa and other African languages, we were astonished to find young men in John Lennon glasses and hair down their backs walking around in long velvet jackets. The campus was alight with demonstrations against Dow Chemical, with antiwar protests. Soon C. was letting his hair grow and I was wearing miniskirts and dangling earrings. We made friends and before long were going to parties unlike any we'd known. We listened to Dylan, danced to "Let's Spend the Night

Together," tirelessly talked politics: Vietnam, Baldwin's essays, women's rights. A friend who was reading Sylvia Plath gave me a copy of Virginia Woolf's *A Room of One's Own*. Our third daughter was born and C. and I returned to Africa for a year, this time to Niger, north of Nigeria, where Hausa was widely spoken: we hadn't forgotten our trip from Igbobi up to Kano during the harmattan, sand moving forward in waves, the pull of the desert. It was in Niger, that year, I turned thirty. By the time we were back in Madison and C. was writing his dissertation on Hausa proverbs, I'd determined to read Proust and write a dissertation of my own. So it was that C. cared for our children while I took the required courses all in a rush and planned to write my dissertation later, after he'd found a job and we'd all moved away from Madison. Many things had come to be that we'd never imagined at all.

And yet how, on the basis of crossing paths in the Scuola di San Giorgio degli Schiavoni with Diana, did she and I find our way immediately on sitting down together to a discussion of whether or not affairs were possible in marriage? How was the subject broached and by whom? But she had married in her early twenties, as had I, and she told me that she and her friends had endlessly discussed the possibilities just as we did now. She did not give advice, did not say how she herself had addressed these difficulties, but, as I nervously gobbled cucumber sandwiches, led me to understand that she believed people had the right to claim some area of privacy around themselves, some measure of freedom wherein the choices they made need not be revealed to anyone at all. She said that fidelity in marriage was not easily defined, that she thought it a strenuous and lifelong enterprise, but that she considered it dirty-minded—that was the expression she used: it rests in my journal—to make fidelity a matter of whether you slept with someone other than your spouse. She said also that she remembered a time not so very long before the afternoon we were speaking when a group of their friends, married couples of the same age, had been talking about these things, and that it had been the women who seemed most to have regretted the opportunities left unexplored. She was not telling me one thing or another, but she was assuring me of the possibility of choice.

In fact, we returned to this subject over a period of several visits spanning the next two years. We talked, too, about our parents and brothers and sisters, and when I voiced a fear that something I was thinking about writing might prove upsetting to someone in my family, she said she thought it best to assume a generosity of response, that that was best for one's own sake and for everyone else's. The subject was quickly dropped, but years later, when we were both writing memoirs, we would return to this subject with greater urgency. She talked, too, about how it was only in her thirties that, like myself, she had come to writing; how, after an extended illness had led her to abandon all hope of a singing career, she had watched Lionel like a hawk to see what his response would be the day she first proposed writing reviews for *The Nation*. But he had encouraged her work, she said, always. Coming down the hall from the back of the apartment, he would courteously greet us on his way out to teach a class, pausing to arrange with her some small errand, a trip to the post office, or a stop at the butcher's to pick up the chicken breasts they would have that night for dinner. Did he have enough money with him? "But don't leave me penniless, Li!"

Diana in 1974 was at work on a review of Nigel Nicolson's *Portrait of a Marriage*, and she said that although she admired the devoted friendship between Vita Sackville-West and Nicolson, she thought their freedoms to live as they liked had largely to do with their privileged position in English society. Members of the middle or working class, pursuing a life as sexually adventurous as theirs, would have paid heavily, both socially and economically. She spoke of the arduous labor writing was for her. She had already asked me if I didn't think Lionel's style sounded simple. "But you can't imagine the . . ." she said, pausing. "Pain?" I offered. "The pain," she repeated, "that went into it." Perhaps it was on this occasion that I complained about how slowly my dissertation was taking shape, because my difficulty prompted a letter dated February 27, 1975:

> "I've been thinking of what you told me of your slowness as a writer; as I said, we're similarly afflicted in this household. I think the important point about which you have to be ruthlessly honest is the matter of progress: do you inch *along*, do you carry the work *forward* if only a small amount at a time? There is no other criterion, it seems to me, for distinguishing between a perhaps too great but nonetheless valuable precision of style and the use of meticulousness as an evasion to be thought of as *only* a problem against which you must mobilize all your energies of self-correction. Once you work out the style for a piece of writing, appropriate to the material and your image of yourself as author, you should, in a morning of work, have a page that's new—that's a practical minimum at your age and stage, I think. Thus, if you go *back* over four or five pages, you should come out with five or six, perhaps not every single day, but most days. Do you manage that? If you do not, then just by force of will you must move on despite this or that lax sentence or this or that insufficient word. Anyway, I'm making this my rule, even at my age and stage, and invite you to join with me."

"Mobilize all your energies of self-correction." I knew the ring of a sentence like this one. But I had heard it at school only in admonitory statements in regard to the prescribed duties of young girls, of married women in relation to their husbands and children. To people you could do something for. I had not yet heard diction such as this used in regard to responsibilities toward oneself or one's chosen work. Nor had anyone ever taken my writing quite so seriously.

Diana would tell me not long before she died that she hadn't seen my face in years. I was startled because it was easy to forget, watching her move quickly across a room, that she could at last see only the edges of things. But startled, too, because I realized she had not seen my face grow older as I had seen hers, that she perhaps imagined mine to be the one that had hovered beside her own years before while she filled my cup with tea as quickly as I drained it, dropping a lump of sugar into it with silver tongs, tearing open a pink slip of saccharine for herself. Or, I wondered, was it, in any case, continuity that we always see in our friends? Did the new lines in their faces finally make very little difference? What mattered was what I could see before me: the woman who at ninety threw her arm, just as she had always done, across the back of the sofa, who sat at ease with her legs apart or with an ankle resting elegantly on a knee. Here she was, bending to pick up the phone as she had during those years when I eagerly listened to her strategies for making sure of her working time. "Yes, yes. I'd adore a visit. That would be wonderful. Next week and the one following are impossible, but would the week after that suit you? Are you quite sure that would fit your schedule? Be really convenient? Good, and in the meantime I'll look forward immensely to our visit."

So that I had wondered if the person on the other end of the line had hung up thinking that it was he or she who had chosen a time one month hence for the visit they had hoped to arrange for the next days.

༄

During the fall of 1975, when Diana and Lionel returned
from their summer away, Lionel was not well and went
into Columbia Presbyterian Hospital for tests. One day in
September I was driving Diana up Riverside Drive to visit
him when she told me that the day before a shadow had
been discovered on his pancreas, a tumor. I thought of the
Guermantes receiving Swann's news that he would soon be
dead: "Why, you'll outlive us all," the duke cries, and sends
up for the red shoes. In the silence that gathered in the closed
spaces of the car, I was made aware by the presence at my side
that for the moment there was nothing to be said and instead
stared mutely through the windshield at the rain-drenched
road. Diana went on to say that he had heard the diagnosis
and that she'd assumed he'd understood until she heard him
later on the phone telling someone that this was all going to
delay his teaching for a couple of weeks.

And then she continued that she knew something had been
wrong in July when he'd had a series of terrible nightmares.
That she blamed herself for thinking so long that the disorder
was psychological and had tried to talk him out of his distress.
I had still found nothing to say when we pulled up in front of
the hospital and she climbed out of the car and disappeared
through the revolving doors.

In one of our visits soon after his death two months later, on
November 5, she said the genius of marriage was that in a
cold world there was one other person for whom you counted
first. When night came, you at last went home to each
other. You might disagree, endure periods of disharmony,
but when one of you was in danger or very unhappy, the

other one rallied. "If Lionel were alive, I know we'd fight sometimes, just as when he was alive. It's not that I think things would be altered to perfection. But he'd be *here*." We were sitting in her immaculate little kitchen, eating tunafish sandwiches. For the moment, the formality of the teas had been put aside. "The world may be lamenting the death of the literary critic," she continued, "but I miss the man bringing home the pork chops."

Out of the corner of my eye, I had been watching a cockroach make a slow path down the wall next to the table where we sat. Just then he crawled into sight. Diana looked blank for a moment, then threw back her head, helplessly delighted with the absurdity of it all. "What a life!" she hooted, as if all our dilemmas were nothing.

In the years following Lionel's death, Diana plunged into the editorial work of putting together his uncollected writing, of seeing his collected work brought out in a new edition, and into writing a book of her own. I, having at last finished my dissertation, began teaching full time. Our afternoons together were less frequent. Sometimes C. and I would be invited for dinner or for drinks, as in the days when Lionel was alive, but Diana was afraid of heights and wasn't eager to come to our fourth-floor apartment. One day she called to say she wanted to make some tapes—informal conversations—in which she talked about her life, and asked if I would be willing to help her do this. We arranged a time, sat in our accustomed places on the sofa, set the tape running, and attempted our usual conversation. But it was all flat and stilted, the rhythms were wrong, and we gave up in defeat.

Then one afternoon in the fall of 1986, when we were again sitting at tea, she told me that her eyesight had in the past few months badly deteriorated. She talked about the ways her life was consequently made more difficult. She needed to bring in more money from her writing now in order to pay the secretary she had recently hired to take dictation. She could no longer see the typewritten page without the aid of a magnifying glass. But her greatest regret, she said, was that she would never again read Proust. I listened amazed. It was ten years since I had completed my dissertation, and over the last months I'd been visited by the thought more and more insistently that it was time to return to Proust. I wanted to read his novel under circumstances that would have nothing to do with a dissertation. I was writing fiction now, and knew I would read *À La Recherche* differently. What's more, the disposal of my time was more or less my own. Our youngest daughter was in her first year of college, C. and I ate our dinner late. So it was quickly agreed. Once a week in the afternoon I would read aloud to us *À La Recherche du Temps Perdu*—in English, of course—an undertaking we could not have predicted would take us six years to complete.

II

Perhaps because Proust's novel begins with an account of that floating state between dream and waking, it soon occurred to me that reading aloud to someone you love is a little like sitting with them in the dark, talking. The words of the book, the image that passes before your eyes, is the dream from which you slowly awaken to find yourself awash in scattered images from your past, odd bits of ponderings for which there seem no words. But if someone is there beside you, and if there are rings of quiet surrounding anything that is said, then these fragments may find their way into speech. Your thoughts can roam freely, darting backward and forward in time, the way they do when you are alone. You are speaking to the dark. Silences, as under a night sky, open to a place beyond themselves.

The book, with Diana, was our dark place, the fertile ground of memory and confidence. Had it ever happened to either of us, as to the narrator when he first encounters Gilberte at Tansonville, that an exchange of eyes had been enough, that it had seemed as if everything had been accomplished in a gaze? Yes, once to her after her mother's death on a boat going to Brazil, when she had been traveling with her father. She had been singing one night to an assembled group and a man had come and stood in the door to listen. She would never forget his face. I had passed someone on a street in a village in southern France, in Provence, when I was twenty-six and we had both stared in instant, blinding recognition. And cruelty such as that with which Françoise had tormented the pregnant kitchen maid, the spring of the asparagus? Yes, we had each encountered that in our childhoods, the sudden revelation of gratuitous malice in an adult, and remembered the thrill of fear it produced.

Or, when we reached *Swann in Love*, Diana confessed she had never been subject to obsessive love, the kind Swann felt for Odette, what she supposed was called romantic love. It was not part of her makeup and she never quite understood what people meant when they talked about it. To be imprisoned in this way! To be sapped of one's will! It made her think of people she had known in the grip of alcohol, or drugs. But there we differed. Love of this kind was all too familiar to me, and I suddenly understood that our conversations about affairs so many years before must have had a different meaning for each of us not apparent at the time. Yet the period had passed for speaking of these things between us.

There were moments, too, many of them, when we sat in hushed and humbled silence. These occurred early in our reading, but were repeated again and again throughout the years. They were almost always in response to a passage building rhythmically, irresistibly, toward a moment of revelation—as, for example, the famous passage in which the taste of the madeleine dipped in tea is said to evoke a joy in the narrator that stirs him from lethargy to the work of memory, the resurrection of the whole of Combray, "town and gardens alike." It was then that we were together listening to the voice beneath the voice on the page, the strains of rapture that are the most intimate thing we know about a writer, the secret urgings of spirit. And it was then I remembered the cathedral at Amiens and the soaring sense of expectation roused by my own uncertain pronunciation of the name of the town, *Cambrai.*

We had begun, rather self-consciously, sitting side by side as usual on the sofa. But before long, as we gradually fell under the spell of words and silence, I found myself in a chair on the other side of the room, facing Diana across a distance. Perhaps we said the light would be better if I sat there, but the light had nothing to do with it. A listener needs room to be alone in the expanding world of the story. And a voice telling a story requires space if it is to assume the anonymity of a voice crying in the wilderness, requires at least the illusion of speaking beyond time and place. It must not be burdened too emphatically with individual history.

And yet, very soon, I found this to be impossible. What could I do when I heard myself reading in the voice my mother had used reading to me as a child, the voice, mimicking her, I had used to read to my own children? I heard the same intonations, the same pauses and emphases, the same strains of irrepressible sadness. Diana's father had been born in the Warsaw ghetto, my mother's grandmother had been born in Ireland during the Famine. Yet here was Diana, and here was I, sitting in an apartment on Claremont Avenue, each listening to Proust read in accents that were beyond our choosing, either hers or mine. And perhaps, for that reason, in a voice after all with its own share of anonymity, the voice of ancestors whose sorrows might find their unlikely but entirely fitting expression in the pages of Proust.

III

It was sometime during those early years when we were reading Proust together, Diana and I, that on my way home one winter's afternoon I paused to watch the setting sun. I often ran the few blocks east to Morningside Drive from sheer exhilaration. But on this December day—turning onto 120th Street from Claremont, looking back toward the Hudson, just beyond the silver tops of the trees in Riverside Park—I stopped, as if recalled to something. The red winter sun was setting, disappearing into the dark Palisades above the icy river. The cold was intense and I continued on my way. But that night I woke from what may have been a dream, or perhaps not a dream at all but a floating reverie.

I seemed to recall, there in the dark, a time when our mother read to us in the late afternoons. It was winter and my brother Charlie and I were sitting on a little sofa, facing a window, one on either side of her. She was reading from a book with a cover the color of dull gold. It was not a book at all, not as

I understand books now, though I know it was Dickens's *A Christmas Carol.* Rather it was a voice, and that voice was hers. She was speaking as if the words were prayers, as if she wanted us to hear in the words something we couldn't see. Her voice was both tender and sorrowful. She pronounced the words as if she herself had known the sufferings of the lonely and the poor, those chilled to the bone, had heard the voices of the afflicted, the wailing in the night. The sun shot down through the trees. It was melting in the branches, it was falling out of sight. Then she stopped reading and stood up and turned on the light above our heads, a bulb skirted by a glass shade. When she sat down again and continued reading, the bright band of red was gone and there was only a shiny black window, the electric light swimming in it.

I may have drifted back to sleep, may even have slept awhile, dreaming of the red sun setting over the Palisades not far away from Diana's, of that winter sunset long ago when our mother's voice had taught us what to listen for. But a little later I woke again, this time to a pounding heart. A nameless anxiety had taken hold, a sense of terrifying urgency. But none of the worries that ordinarily preoccupied me seemed to fit. In this case, I was being recalled to something of a different order. It seemed that from every side I heard a soft hissing, something like the sound of snow driving forward in a storm against a wall or window or tower, blotting out the familiar landmarks and signposts, leaving behind mysterious shapes that rendered the mind blank and stupid. I couldn't make out a thing.

And then, thinking of nothing at all, I understood: I must change my life. I must change my life. In spite of the many things my life had included, and I didn't stop to name them,

I'd nevertheless missed the most important thing of all: the pearl of great price. There wasn't a moment to lose. And I faintly discerned, in the reverberating silence that followed, that I would discover what that was only if—as Miss Hughes had instructed us so many years ago—I was able, with all the attention she had insisted on, to listen for the vibrations of what had come before and prepare for those that would follow. But that night and its urgency disappeared like a dream erased and I wouldn't think of it again for a while.

IV

Diana was eighty-one when we began our readings. The novel was long. She had already told me that when you were as old as she, you did not expect to live for more than a few years. That expectation, she said, both had its reality and did not. And yet, perhaps because we had entered the sphere of timelessness in which the book revolves, perhaps because the words we were reading were proof against the destruction of our present, the fear of time running out did not intrude until the book was closed at the end of each afternoon and returned to its place on the table next to the sofa. We were at first making use of the little Scott-Moncrieff volumes, taken from a shelf in the dining room, that had Lionel's tracings in them—a pencil line drawn next to selected passages ending in an arrow turned in at the bottom—and when we completed one volume we left it on the table for the next to rest on. After we had changed to the Kilmartin translation, each volume wrapped in silver paper eventually took its place on top of all the others. There was, then, a vivid growing testimony to the accumulation of our afternoons, at times a comfort of sorts, at others a bleak reminder that someday it would all be over—the book, the afternoons, Diana and I sitting together reading with our cups of tea beside us.

But there would be occasions when the minutes passed one by one. The open-air charms of Combray and Balbec behind us, we found ourselves moving laboriously through the corridors of *The Guermantes Way.* Then, just as reading aloud had earlier been the occasion for a sharing of wonders, the sound of my own voice seemed a hindrance to understanding. I could not let my eye run quickly ahead, as when reading alone, to see what was there and move on. Nor reread a sentence or paragraph meditatively, pausing to reflect, and afterward turn the next pages rapidly. Every word had to be pronounced, each given its due. Sometimes I would turn a page and fall into a stupor, appalled by the prospect of a block of print unbroken by a single paragraph, only to sneak a glance at the pages immediately following and find they were the same. Then the reading seemed a chore. Intent, simply, on looking ahead to locate the end of the sentence so that I wouldn't heedlessly run up against it, as against a brick wall, I found myself struggling to understand what it was all about and, when Diana interrupted with a comment, was relieved to be able to stop for a rest.

We had made our stolid way through a long account of the afternoon reception given by Madame de Villeparisis and were embarked on a dinner party at the Guermantes when Diana broke in to wonder aloud if they would ever get to the table. And then again when we were told at last they had, because we weren't given any details besides an unspecified bowl of soup, to conjecture what they were eating.

After we had concocted a meal for them, Diana asked me

what I was having for dinner that night, and I asked her the same question. We then talked about soups and how we both liked cold summer soups in particular. I recounted to her my experiment with cucumber soup at Igbobi College, using powdered milk. She in turn told me she sometimes served a cold asparagus soup with sliced cucumber on top that she liked very much, and I described a curried pea soup thickened with half-and-half or yogurt. We wrote down the recipes. Our conversation ran next to summer itself, and when I told her that we had decided to rent a house in the country, we spoke of visitors. We agreed we loved the idea of having people come to stay; it answered to some idea of bounty and life at high tide. "But visitors are the despair of work," she told me solemnly. "I warn you about this. If you leave your doors wide open, you'll spend all your time in the kitchen and changing beds. I had to learn this myself during our years in Westport."

Edith Wharton, in contrast, I reminded Diana, with a house full of guests, had spent her mornings in bed writing, scattering the sheets of paper on the floor where they were later collected by a secretary who typed them up. She had a complete staff to take care of things, no children to tend, could do her work and enjoy her visitors in the afternoon. "But wouldn't you want to know what they were all doing?" Diana asked. "You'd be in bed, and they'd be downstairs talking to each other, happy without you."

We pondered this dilemma for a while and then Diana said that one of Edmund Wilson's wives, so that he might not be disturbed, would bring him his lunch on a tray adorned with a flower stuck in a vase. Lionel had been exactly the opposite. He'd leave the door of his study open so that Jim could run in and out at any time, and he did, to Lionel's delight; the cats would settle on the keys of his typewriter and he would work around them.

We talked of the Carlyles, of Jane and Thomas, and how she never got to her work at all, ever. Diana said Jane had spent her life protecting him, as he sat writing in Chelsea, from the noise of the renovators who were soundproofing the house, that she had almost pleaded with the roosters not to crow. I asked her if she knew the story of Alfred de Musset and George Sand, how waking early in the morning, he had thought that George Sand, disheveled with sleep, already bent by the fire over her writing desk, had not presented a very attractive image to his eyes.

For a moment there was silence from across the room. Then, in a burst: "Kill 'em all! Shoot 'em dead!"

Another pause: "And what kind of an image, pray, did *he* present?"

Each of us, separately, was engaged as well in her own struggle with the clock. Diana had already been writing for some time the memoir that became *The Beginning of the Journey;* and I—after a return to Niger—had begun to write something that, although fiction, was close enough to memoir to provoke some of the same concerns. I'd been visiting a daughter who had herself returned to Niger to work for a couple of years in a place she remembered from childhood. Now Diana and I were both laboring to get our words on paper. And Diana was also struggling with difficulties new to her. It was, she said, not only that words didn't come to her as quickly as they had when she was younger but that dictating to a secretary was a tricky business. The person receiving the words on the other side of the table—whether through some attitude of sympathy or the lack of it—made a difference in what she was able to express. But even more pressingly, she was fearful that in speaking of Lionel as she had known him, and of their marriage, she would be perceived as irreverent or disloyal. She said that Lionel would have urged her to speak out, that he would have taken courage from her trying to tell the truth. She went on to say that everyone had always tried to make so much of her being married to someone more gifted than herself. "But I absolutely loved it," she said. "I ate it up."

I reminded her of what, years before, she had advised in response to my own difficulties—that one must try to assume generosity on the part of one's readers. I said, too, how disheartening it was to read about a life that was presented as seamless, how one could only find hope, apparently, in the reflection of troubles recognizable as one's own. I was speaking partly to give myself courage, prey to some of the same fears as she was. I had read many accounts of the connection between mothers and daughters, but almost every one of them had been written by a daughter. I hoped that my own dilemmas and guilts and confusions as well as my joys would be recognized by someone else. When I told Diana I had begun to give one or two people portions to read of my own work in progress, I saw her face change. "If you give your work to someone," she said, "it's impossible to control the response." She warned me that I should be very careful, that response in the wrong place can set you back. I said I had taken this step because working in the dark a long time was so difficult. "Be patient, darling," she said. "Be strong."

After we had sat in silence for a moment, I asked, already knowing the answer, if life was any less turbulent when you were older. "It isn't for me," she answered. "And I don't think it will be for you." Then, as we were standing at the door, I at last in my coat about to leave: "I think we're only half committed to reading Proust. We have to have our weekly dose of talk."

❦

We had at last left the Guermantes behind and embarked on *The Cities of the Plains*, plunging into the story of the narrator's love for Albertine. His love, like Swann's, is volatile, painfully attuned to absence, to anguished fears that the lover might be cherishing secret desires for someone else. But the inner world of the lover remains closed. After listening to an analysis of jealousy drawn out over many pages, Diana said how absurd it all was, how by contrast with the simplicities of Combray it was all too much, simply too much.

I remarked that I thought this an element of Proust's genius; he risked absurdity, took things to the last length. Diana said nothing for a moment. "You're right," she said at last. "You're absolutely right. And that's my despair. My own writing doesn't do that." She had been rereading the memoir that now was almost finished and had decided that it was the public story. "But there's another story yet to be told. My own. The texture of my days isn't there."

She said for example that once when she was a young girl she'd been walking with her father down on 18th Street. A man had approached, asking for money, and her father had reached into his pocket and given him a quarter. As they continued on their way, Diana had looked back over her shoulder and seen the man walk across the street and into a bar. Diana had asked her father, then, what was the point of giving the man a quarter if he were only going to buy a drink with it. "He needs that drink more than I need my quarter," her father had replied.

"But where do I put that?" Diana said. "I can't just thrust the story in anywhere, it has to have a place. What does it mean?"

I told her I thought Proust himself must have struggled with all this, that the manuscripts I'd seen in Paris, the week following our meeting in Venice, had revealed his confusion. There had been one bound notebook, I remembered, in which page after page of small legible handwriting, all in sequence, had been struck out with a firm line of black ink drawn diagonally from top to bottom.

All discarded. But also carefully preserved in case he should reconsider or wish to make use of them later, in another context. I told her, too, about the drawings in the margins, the doodlings, the woman in a long dress leaning on a parasol, and the railroad tracks, wide at the bottom, that running up the side of the page had narrowed to infinity.

Before long we'd arrived at that remarkable section in the same volume called "The Intermissions of the Heart." The narrator is visiting Balbec a second time and, on arriving at the Grand Hotel, is bending down in the quiet of his room to take off his boots when he is overwhelmed by the recollection of his grandmother years before kneeling lovingly, humbly at his feet, assisting him in the same task. At once he is shaken by sobs. He has scarcely missed her; she has been dead a year and this is the first time her lost presence has broken in on him. Adding to his misery is the knowledge that he had inflicted senseless injuries on her, mocking her when she had posed for a photograph that she had secretly intended as a memento for him after her death. His mother's mourning, so different from his own, is constant, irreversible.

As always when Proust is speaking from the place of wondering discovery, the rhythms of the sentences had changed and Diana and I sat breathlessly as the room filled with the cadences of a nameless grief. At the end of the passage my voice came to a halt.

Neither of us said a word. It was late October and already the luminous fanfare of ginkgo leaves was being swallowed by twilight. I was about to continue reading when Diana broke the silence. She said that beneath the narrator's comparisons of his own superficial grief for his grandmother with his mother's consuming sorrow she had heard some fear that he had never loved anyone in his whole life. "And I don't think I have either," she said.

For herself, she continued, she thought this incapacity had a kind of Freudian origin; her passionate love for her father had been refused and she had never been able to offer it again. She'd had only a glimpse of this possibility in all her years of analysis, but she thought nonetheless that it was true. Then she went on to say that although she thought she had herself never loved anyone, she'd never known anyone else who had either. Devotion: she'd seen plenty of that, how in the case of a couple she knew one cared for the other who had suffered from a stroke, cutting his meat, helping him up from a chair. But this wasn't what she meant by love, any more than she meant Swann's obsessive love for Odette, or the narrator's for Albertine. No, what she was talking about was the passionate attachment, the fixed attention over time, the blaze that would brook no replacement.

We wondered, then, whether it was this undying love that everyone pined for, feeling in its absence that we alone had remained on the outside looking in, never having experienced what we are pleased to call life, watching others and envying them, imagining everyone else had known something we ourselves had not; whether we were all haunted by the fear that we had never lived, not really, that there was something we had missed, something waiting, even calling to us, that we had looked straight through without ever recognizing.

After sitting in silence some moments, Diana got up to draw the white curtains on the night. The phone rang and, after she'd promised to call back later on and hung up, I resumed reading, pursuing the slow tale of the narrator's unraveling grief in Balbec. But we hadn't got very far before we broke off to remember, at a distance of almost twenty years, our meeting in Venice.

"We picked each other up," she said. "No," she corrected herself, "you picked *me* up, there on the steps of the Schiavoni." We recalled our lunch together, the icy beer and sandwiches, but she didn't remember that she had talked about staying with her father at the Danieli or that she had invited me to stop at the hotel. When I had seen them at the coffee bar the morning I was leaving Venice, I told her, I had used the fact that I'd stumbled on the Danieli as a pretext to greet her, that Proust, who had stayed at the same hotel with his mother, like his narrator, had been present even then. "If you hadn't stopped in the coffee bar we'd have never seen each other again. It would have been only another Venetian interlude."

The air of intimacy was gathering in the room, the air of two people drawing close. I felt myself reeling away in terror, fearful of the presence of love. "I'm not good at expressing gratitude," she said, "but I can never tell you what these afternoons mean to me, how important a part of my life they have become."

I told her then that if I lived to be as old as she was now, I knew that these years of our reading together week after week would return to me.

She paused a moment. "Do you mean," she asked—and here she spoke tentatively, carefully—"do you mean, perhaps, that you might think of me, I don't know, but perhaps as some kind of a model?"

"I'm sure I will," I answered, "but no, that wasn't what I meant. It's rather that I'll be warmed by the knowledge that I've *had* this experience, that it will always be mine, however old I become."

And then I saw in a flash—imagining myself when I was perhaps as old as Diana was now, looking back at the two of us from some faraway point in time sitting here in the twilight with the lamp and book between us—that the life we'd been talking about, the life denied us, was a creature of the air, a fancy, a way of giving a shape, a story, to the lives we'd been given: lives too various, too mysterious, too fluid in complexity and surprise to make sense of. And seeded too with death, with the end of things. In my own, for all time, amid so much else, a boy sat listening one snowy afternoon to a requiem, his head buried in his arms, and a class of children were instructed they must never forget that for someone else's sorrow they must reserve their deepest bow.

The unlived life was the shadow against which our actual lives trembled and shook, the shadow that revealed the color and shape of what we had. We'd been talking, Diana and I, of our own fear—and the fear of so many others—that we alone were incapable of love, that we alone were excluded from the feast of life. I remembered my own terror when I was still young that books would deprive me of ordinary joys and sorrows, that my incessant reading disguised a fear of striking out. But here I was, so many years later, and it was once again the book Diana and I were reading together that was bringing in the news.

Looking back at the two of us from some imagined point in the future, I could see that it was these moments together that had themselves been what my dream had named the pearl of great price, the life we'd actually lived, the pages we'd turned together these many afternoons.

V

There were days when I would arrive and Diana would say she was a little tired, would I mind if she put her head down on the pillow of the sofa while I read. She would tell me that if she fell asleep I was to let her know. She would close her eyes, then, and after some time had gone by without any sound in the room except that of my own voice droning on, when I had just decided she had probably fallen asleep and was asking myself what I should do, suddenly there would be a splash, as with a whale rising from the deep, and she would exclaim that this was a remarkable passage, what he had to say about his mother's refusal of a kiss and Albertine's displeasure was absolutely accurate, they both drew from the same source. Or, instead, in a different mode, she might suddenly, vigorously, declare that she didn't believe a word of it, that here he had taken a wrong turn.

But one afternoon, when she was feeling unwell enough to have remained in bed and I was sitting in a chair in her bedroom, a silence continued longer than I had ever remembered it. I was reading the passage in which the narrator hears Albertine's window flung open in the middle of the night and, in a fit of anguish, paces up and down in the corridor outside her room, vainly hoping that the sound of his footsteps will attract her attention. I continued to read on, but this time Diana did not stir. Facing me, on the bureau, were photographs of Lionel and Jim. A Blake engraving hung on the wall nearby. Beyond the room stretched the long hallway lined with books and at one end the *OED* on its stand, which I had often consulted when we weren't sure of a word. The apartment was moving from light to dark, and when my voice came to a tentative halt I knew I was sitting in the silence that surrounded Diana every night when she turned off the lights.

Perhaps to keep myself from imagining too closely what that silence might hold, I resumed reading, and when Diana stirred at last I was just finishing the volume that concludes with Albertine's rising early one morning and disappearing from the narrator's life before he is awake.

But there was another occasion on which Diana, alert in her accustomed place on the sofa, one arm flung across its back, the other at rest on the arm beside her, listened to page after page without speaking. The narrator is describing the astonishing masquerade he walks into at the reception of the Prince de Guermantes, where he has expected to find old friends. The people he has not seen for many years are unrecognizable to him—as, indeed, he finds to his surprise, is he to them. Diana listened in silence to the long descriptions of the horrors wrought on faces by time, of the parade of grotesque figures, the puppets, into which the friends of his youth have been transformed. There came, then, a passage in which an old woman receives the news of the death of a contemporary not with sadness but with the satisfaction of a victor: the other is dead, but she is still alive. She feels she has triumphed.

The room had been still for so long that I had wondered

if Diana would speak only when the book was closed for the afternoon. But now, into the unbroken quiet, sounded a long, deep "No."

"No," Diana repeated after a moment. "That's not the way it is. I used to imagine the same thing myself when Lionel's mother would talk about the death of someone belonging to her own generation. I used to think that what she felt was vindication. But I was wrong: it's not like that at all. Desperation is what you feel. You watch one friend after another removed and there's not a thing you can do about it. Nothing. You feel absolutely desperate. To imagine you feel triumph is the mistaken idea of a younger person. I remember thinking that myself. Poor Proust didn't live long enough to know."

It was winter now and the ginkgo tree appeared nubby at the window, its limbs in the dim afternoon light curving like the neck of a dinosaur, a swan. We sat in silence, I marveling that although I had come across this passage in my earlier readings of Proust, it had never occurred to me to question its authority. And yet this was not the first time, with Diana, that I had hesitated before reading aloud a scene in which an older person figured. It was scarcely that Proust was lacking in imagination; it was rather that he had died in his early fifties. We at last took up the book to hear the aging Odette described as sitting a little out of the way while people, thinking she couldn't hear a word, loudly tell each other not to bother speaking to her, that she is completely beyond it all, that no one need take the trouble any longer to introduce themselves or inquire after her.

"It's not the disabilities of age that are so painful," Diana broke in. "It's the indignities. One is treated as if one no longer had a wit in one's head. It's truly maddening. The fact of age, it seems, disqualifies one for ordinary exchange."

She sat thoughtfully for a moment, then threw one of the glances across the room that made it so difficult to remember that she was almost blind. "You know the three stages of life, don't you? I never told you this one? Well, there's youth, middle age, and finally 'you're looking wonderful.'"

I laughed and she continued. "Sometimes I wish someone would tell me I look like an old witch. Then at least I'd know I were still in life." She paused, considering. "But sometimes, too, people my own age make me want to scream. Someone calls and says they saw something or other in the paper about the past, that they know that's all we really care about now, the things that happened in our youth. What can this possibly mean? I want to scream. I don't know why it upsets me so much."

I told her, then, how my mother, who Diana knew was dying of cancer, went on with the life she had always led, going through the round of her days, inviting people for dinner, working in her garden.

"What an affirmation!" Diana said.

"Of what?" I asked stupidly, wanting her to spell it out.

"Of life!" she said. "Your mother has not given up on life. She is holding to the things that have always been hers, to what she is."

Then, after another long moment of reflection: "I wonder if it is an act of will that keeps her going, or if it is something innate."

I didn't altogether understand the distinction: it seemed that the "something innate" might include an act of will. So, wanting her to elaborate, I asked what she thought it was for herself. Was it will, was it determination, that made the difference in her life?"

"No," she said. "I never ask myself, when I wake up in the morning, if I'll have the courage for today. It's simply my nature to go on as I do, it's the way that I am." And then, returning to my mother: "She's carrying on with her work." There was another pause, followed a moment later by the words I'd heard her pronounce more than once before: "It's our work that saves us."

The end of the book had swung sharply into view. Each week I would tell Diana how many pages we still had to read; we were preparing ourselves for the voice to fall silent that had accompanied us through six years. "I feel as if I'm dropping off a precipice," Diana said, and then one day in January, when it seemed we might finish that day, I told her we had only seven more pages to read. We at once began and when we had arrived at the last paragraphs I was unsure whether to break in to tell her so or to allow the rhythm of the sentences to carry us like a wave to shore. I could see, but she could not, that we had only two paragraphs remaining and then had arrived at the last sentence of all: "But at least, if strength were granted me for long enough to accomplish my work, I should not fail, even if the result were to make them resemble monsters, to describe men first and foremost as occupying a place, a very considerable place compared with the restricted one which is allotted to them in space, a place on the contrary immoderately prolonged—for simultaneously, like giants plunged into the years, they touch epochs that are immensely far apart, separated by the slow accretion of many, many days—in the dimension of Time."

I had always imagined that when we reached the final word, the room would reverberate, that all our afternoons would, like the novel we had read, immediately assume the irrevocable shape of a completed work. But the silence that followed was open, answerable to the next. Diana looked up expectantly, and in response I told her we had reached the end. We sat there in silence for a few moments, and then began to speak of the abounding wealth of these so many afternoons. How during these years we had been writing our own books and how Proust's voice had been present throughout it all, seductive, tedious, rapt. We spoke of how that voice finally seemed one's own lost voice, the voice of one's deepest self, how the narrator's memories at last seemed to belong to a life one had known long ago. And I silently remembered the warm autumn afternoons among the chrysanthemums on the steps of the house in Avesnes and how those moments had once seemed to me to belong to some earlier, forgotten life.

"And even so we haven't been a bit solemn, have we," Diana said.

When I finally got up to leave, we stood at the door, looking back at the pile of books on the table by the sofa. "Goodbye, dear Proust," I called out. "Goodbye."

"We love you, Proust," she called, and then, turning to me: "How silly we are. But at least it's just the two of us."

And yet, if not in the moment, at least in the weeks that followed we found the book had indeed set its seal on the years. We had thought to read next a book that could not possibly invite comparison, that was as far away from *À La Recherche du Temps Perdu* as we could make it. Half in joking one of us suggested *Little Women*, a book neither had read since childhood. And yet, after the astringency of Proust, we discovered that Alcott's book was, as Diana pronounced it, "treacle," better left to children. We tried one novel and then another, Cather's *A Lost Lady*, Wharton's *The*

Age of Innocence, but the long afterglow cast by our hours with Proust left us restless, easily dissatisfied. Was it because we would have thought ourselves disloyal to have fallen so soon into the embrace of another novelist? Or because our imaginations, deeply stained in the colors of Proust, were for the moment impervious? When we happened on Jane Austen's *Persuasion*, a book about passionate attachment enduring over time, we were for the first time captivated. But in our new fascination we could not help feeling a stab of regret.

My mother died that fall, and a few weeks later Diana inquired about my father, who, having just turned ninety, was only a few months older than herself. She asked how he was doing, and whether I thought he would remarry.

"I hope not!" I burst out. If pressed, I might have admitted that I thought his age disqualified him, as well as his sixty years of marriage to my mother.

Diana sat looking at me and then quietly told me that she didn't know if she had ever before been shocked by anything I had said but that this time she was. Why was it so preposterous an idea that my father marry again? Why should he not? I could see that her response was an outright expression of my own more unspoken outrage, and I sat chastened and silent. Whatever my reasons, she went on to say—and I knew she was thinking with some justification that I had no desire to share my father—I must allow him in any way I could to feel comfortable if he should find someone else, or make efforts in that direction. And I must remember that he had only a very few years in which to do so. I could have no idea, she went on, how lonely it was to be by yourself after sharing a life for so long, that he was only beginning to get the taste of it, that it grew more lonely with time. She said that she herself, in the first years after Lionel's death, had thought remarriage would be an act of disloyalty. "But I have come to feel that I was wrong," she said. "What I imagined to be disloyalty was in fact fear of life."

Then, reflecting, she went on to say that in any case our culture looked on older women's sexual lives very differently from older men's. She thought that most people regarded sexuality in older women with mixed feelings verging on disgust and that this attitude had something to do with the middle-aged seeing their own mothers in elderly women. The whole business was altogether too complicated. Men, by contrast, however old, were regarded more tolerantly, even approvingly. Abiding sexual energies were seen as reassuring evidence of a firm hold on life.

Was it at this moment we spoke of the reviews that were coming out on Diana's memoir that had been published some months before? As she had feared, there were indeed those who disapproved of her discussions of her marriage, thought she needn't have disclosed things Lionel might have preferred left unsaid. "But you know," she said, "every one of these reviews has been written by a man. Not one woman, in reviewing the book, has taken exception with what I said or has charged me with disloyalty. There's a story in that."

Then, as I was getting up to leave: "Too many buttons in life. Too many buttons to button and unbutton."

We at last happened on R. W. B. Lewis's *The Jameses: A Family Narrative*, a book in which we soon realized we might stretch and sprawl. It was both very long and very absorbing and would happily carry us over many months, perhaps even some years. As we turned the pages of the first chapter, however, gripped perhaps by fear of the future, one book after another suddenly occurred to us that we determined to take up when this one was finished. On a small paper, stuck in the last page of the book, I made out the list: a new biography of George Eliot that Diana had heard about, Amy Kelly's life of Eleanor of Aquitaine, Elizabeth Gaskell's of Charlotte Brontë. That taken care of, we let ourselves drop carelessly into the spinning world of the James family, of which Henry was our much-acclaimed hero. "Henry to the rescue!" Diana cried when we heard how, soon after their father's death, he had immediately traveled to Milwaukee to visit his ailing younger brother Wilkie. It had come to light that Wilkie, sorely in need, had been left out of the will altogether, and Henry's response had been to repair, with patient generosity, the wrongs done to his younger brother, corresponding with each member of the family. And we exclaimed approvingly when, as on many occasions, we were led to believe that he alone had been capable of responding to Alice's sufferings with imagination as well as concern. Like the kindly Ralph Touchett to Isabel's, I thought. I had in the intervening years reread *The Portrait of a Lady* but had not suggested the novel when we were looking for something new. Osmond seemed ever more terrible and Isabel's deluded, fatal approach to him all but unbearable.

Diana had already told me that at her age, on arriving at the end of a piece of writing, it was difficult to resist the feeling that one's life's work was over, that one had completed what one was meant to do. But now, in the years following the publication of the memoir, it seemed that ideas for new work rushed in, writing of a more personal nature than formerly, the brimming life she felt had been left out of the earlier reviews and essays. One day she was telling me about the ways holidays had been celebrated when she was a child, and then how during the summers she had gone away to a camp in the Berkshires. "Perhaps I'll write about that," she said. "I haven't begun to explore my childhood."

I remarked how extraordinary it was, the surge of material at this moment in her life. "It couldn't have happened earlier," she said, "Not when Lionel was alive." Perhaps she'd been given to polemical writing at an earlier time, she continued, because she hadn't allowed what was more intuitive, more associative, to emerge for fear of competing with him. That was to have been his sphere. He had wanted to be a novelist; the life of a critic had always seemed to him second best. And until she'd written the memoir, she hadn't been aware that she might one day want to look back to her childhood. They'd talked about their ambitions as they had about everything else, she said, absolutely everything. She could say whatever she liked to him because he never held anything against her. And he'd always said himself that she was underappreciated, that people didn't know her worth.

I answered that his crediting this fact must have made a difference.

"I don't know," she said slowly, musing. "It might have lulled me, made me accept things too easily."

We had come to a place in our book where, in a discussion of Henry James's novel *The Princess Casamassima*, Lewis mentions Lionel's essay by the same name, its brilliance and insight. "Have you ever read that essay?" Diana broke in.

I told her I had, years before.

"He figured it all out from intuition," she said, "and only afterward did the research. He'd come home from the library every day and say quietly, triumphantly, I was right, it *was* that way." Further down the page Lewis went on to explain that although Trilling had got the autobiographical element right, it was Rosie Muniment and not the Princess, as he had supposed, who was based on Alice.

It was disquieting, after Diana's eager account of the manner in which the essay had taken shape, to be floating on the air words that seemed to discredit it. But she listened without comment.

Years earlier Diana had once told me that before Lionel died he had destroyed the early manuscripts of his essays, the ones that showed the extent of her editorial assistance. And perhaps it was on this afternoon, perhaps another soon afterward, that she repeated the story. "I think I told you this once before," she said. I told her I remembered and she went on to say that there may have been reasons for his having destroyed them, that she knew someone had told him that only the latest manuscripts had any value, although she herself couldn't understand why this should be the case. But then, she continued, he hadn't destroyed other early manuscripts, ones she'd had no part in. "It's not a pretty picture," she said.

We sat thinking about this and then she said, after a long pause, that perhaps she had particularly stringent values, that perhaps she extended her censure too readily, on too many fronts, she didn't know.

In the spring of 1996, soon after Diana had been diagnosed with cancer, she returned to the question of judgment. It was an afternoon in May and the ginkgo was in full leaf, casting a green light in the room. The day was warm, almost a summer's day, and we were sipping iced tea. *The Jameses* lay open in my lap, but we were making slow progress. "I have never been able to get over the idea of wanting people to be perfect," Diana said. "And where did I get the idea they should be? I suppose, as in everything, from my family. I'm judgmental, I know that, I've said hard and harsh things, and this has given me a bad reputation in some quarters."

She was sitting on the sofa with her arm extended along the back, wearing a dark blue shirtwaist and blue stockings, her face thoughtful. After our time together she had an appointment for a CAT scan.

"Well," I said at last, "you're full of responses and feelings in regard to people, that's true. And you express them strongly. You say what you think and leave it at that. People are sometimes offended or think you're wrong. But it seems to me that you're also flexible in your judgments. They seem to be changing all the time."

"I hope you'll put that in writing," she replied.

"I will."

Then she told the story of how Eudora Welty had long ago forgiven her. When Diana had first begun to write for *The Nation* in the early 1940s, she had written a review of a collection of Eudora's stories. "I could have put what I wanted to say differently," Diana said. "I needn't have been so harsh. I was just showing off."

Then one Sunday afternoon, years later, perhaps in the late 1950s, a group of her friends and Lionel's had planned to take a picnic to Saxon Woods. It was early summer and there was a rainstorm, so they had all decided to stay in the city. They had spent the afternoon in the apartment, where we were sitting now, getting drunk. Every once in a while someone would run out to buy another bottle while the others, in desperation, rummaged through the cupboards, drinking whatever they could get their hands on. At last, when they were all reeling, Diana remembered that she and Lionel had been invited that night by some friends for dinner. But nobody could move. So she had called and explained the situation. The friends said she needn't worry, Eudora Welty had been with them all afternoon and that they would all come over to Claremont Avenue. Diana had been apprehensive, but when Eudora arrived she had greeted Diana warmly, showing no trace of bitterness. Someone put on a record and they had all leapt from their chairs and begun to dance, Eudora kicking off her shoes. Soon everyone was spinning around the room in tipsy oblivion.

It was on that same afternoon that Diana told me that the strangest thing had happened since she had received her diagnosis. She found that she had been drained of all ambition for herself, she could scarcely remember what it was about. Not the writing itself, but where she would place it, how it would be received. Instead she lay awake at night worrying about her friends' work, wondering how it would fare. This had become her preoccupation and she couldn't shake it.

Diana's "camp story," as she called it, came out that summer in *The New Yorker*. With the money it earned, Diana rented a house in Wellfleet for two months rather than the customary one. I called early in July, the first weekend after she had arrived. The car ride up had done something to her back— the car seats were "not designed for human beings"—and as we spoke she was prone. But from where she was lying she could look through a window and see the green leaves of summer stirring in the sun.

Then she told me about her days. From nine-thirty in the morning until one o'clock, she worked with the help of a secretary. Afterward she was free to have lunch and spend the rest of the afternoon and evening with friends who had come to visit. Her ninety-first birthday was only a couple of weeks away and Jim and his wife and the grandchildren she loved would be with her. "I don't know how people grow old without work," she said. "And writing is the best work of all. You can set up a schedule that will make it a part of every day. And you can take it with you anywhere."

She began to speak again about the lightly moving leaves she could make out on the other side of the window, how they kept her company in the room where she was lying. There were spots of sun there, too, she thought. Or was she remembering the trees of her childhood.

"But you sound radiantly happy!" I exclaimed, thinking how dazzling the light had been on the steps of the Schiavoni and how we had moved away into the shade waiting for us beneath an awning.

"If these are the final months of my life," she answered, "I could not be more so."

We said goodbye then and only later did I understand it had been for the last time.

Acknowledgments

Different parts of this book have been written over time and many people have been present to me. Faithful readers, Mary Gordon, Joan Silber, Louis Asekoff, Myra Goldberg, Jean Valentine, Rob Nixon, Anne McClintock. Elizabeth and Sarah and Kathleen G. Hill have sustained my writing, always, as have my sisters, Mary Safrai and Jane Kuniholm, my brother, Bill Balet. Margot Livesey has been its guardian.

And thanks to Anna Stein, encouraging, persistent, wise, and to Joe Olshan who has faithfully and imaginatively seen these pages through. I'm grateful to the colonies that have supported my work: MacDowell, Yaddo, and Ragdale. And to the monasteries that have given space and welcome: Regina Laudis in Connecticut, New Clairvaux in California. To Mary Ellen Capek and Susan Hallgarth for the shelter of their casita in New Mexico.

The students at Sarah Lawrence College, as well as those at Igbobi College, have read with me and pondered the meanings of many novels, enlarging my understanding.

Ben Waleru and Diana Trilling, constant spirits, remain close. As do my mother who loved the spoken word and my father who loved the written.

Clifford Hill from the first inspired our travels. His imagination seized on possibility. He sought out the stranger, learned his language. My own first reader, custodian of our common memory, to him I dedicate these pages with gratitude and love.

A NOTE ON THE TYPE

This book was set in Walbaum, a typeface designed in 1810 by German punch cutter J.E. Walbaum. Walbaum's type is more French than German in appearance. Like Bodoni, it is a classical typeface, yet its openness and slight irregularities give it a human, romantic quality.

ABOUT THE AUTHOR

Kathleen Hill eaches in the M.F.A. program at Sarah Lawrence College. Her first novel *Still Waters in Niger* was named a notable book by the *New York Times, Los Angeles Times, Chicago Tribune*, and was nominated for the Dublin IMPAC Award. The French translation, *Eaux Tranquilles*, was short-listed for the Prix Femina Étranger. Her second novel *Who Occupies This House* was selected as an Editors' Choice by the *New York Times*. Her stories have appeared in *Best American Short Stories, Pushcart Prize XXV*, and *The Pushcart Book of Short Stories*.

www.kathleenhillwriter.com